Artist Profiles

Columbus, OH

Photo Credits

3 ©Gary Auerbach/Platinum Photographer; 4 ©Corbis/Bettmann; 5 Complimentary Martha Berry; 6 ©AP/Wide World Photos; 7 ©Roger Viollet/Getty Images; 8 ©Beth A. Keiser/AP/Wide World Photos; 9 ©Dominique Berretty/Black Star; 10 ©Laura Platt Winfrey/Woodfin Camp & Associates; 11 ©Scala/Art Resource, NY; 12 ©Pierre Vauthey/Corbis Sygma; 13 ©Getty Images; 14 Royal Library, Turin, Italy. Scala/Art Resource, NY; 15 ©Ralph Morse/Getty Images; 16 Museo del Prado, Madrid, Spain/Scala/Art Resource, NY; 17 Photo by Phil Hossack; 18 ©Ann Chwatsky; 19 Harry Fonseca in his Santa Fe studio with recent works. Photo by Yvonne Bond. Courtesy of the Wheelwright Museum; 20 ©Hulleah Tsinhnahjinnie; 21 ©Belvedere-Tiburon Landmarks Society; 22 ©McMichael Canadian Art Collection Archives. Photo by Robert McMichael; 23 Complimentary Martin O'Neill; 24 ©Brian Seed/Black Star; 25 ©Archive Photo; 26 ©Lisa Rose/Globe Photos; 27 Courtesy Andre Emmerich Gallery; 28 ©Culver Pictures; 29 ©David Sillitoe/Camer Press/Globe Photos; 30 ©Mohamed Mekkawi/Howard University; 31 ©Walter Weisman/Globe Photos; 32 ©Archiv/Interfoto; 33 ©Dan Budnik/Woodfin Camp & Associates; 34 National Museum of Women in the Art, Washington, DC; 35 ©Black Images; 36 Courtesy George Yater/Provincetown Art Association and Museum Collection; 37 Complimentary Nancy Sirkis/Bernice Steinbaum Gallery, Miami, FL; 38 ©Oscar White/Corbis; 39 ©Photothèque R. Magritte-ADAGP / Art Resource, NY; 40 Courtesy of Alexander and Bonin, NY. Photo by Peter Bellamy; 41 ©CNAC/MNAM/Dist. Réunion des Musées Nationaux/Art Resource, NY; 42 ©UPI/Corbis-Bettmann; 43 Complimentary Harrison McIntosh; 44 ©Laurie Platt Winfrey/Woodfin Camp & Associates; 45 ©David Lees/Corbis; 46 Complimentary Ann C. Sherman; 47 ©Ullstein Bilderdienst; 48 Complimentary Joseph Norman; 49 ©Getty Images; 50 ©Timothy Greenfield-Sanders; 51 ©Bettmann/Corbis; 52 ©Smithsonian American Art Museum, Washington, DC/Art Resource, NY; 54 ©Art Resource, NY; 55 ©San Francisco History Center, San Francisco Public Library; 56 ©Suzanne Opton/Courtesy Steinbaum Krauss Gallery; 57 Complimentary Henry Seaweed; 58 Photograph ©1996 Detroit Institute of Arts, Detroit Art Founders Society Purchase, Chaim, Fanny, Louis, Benjamin, Anne, and Florence Kaufman Memorial Trust; 59 ©Thomas Hoepker/Magnum Photos; 60 Courtesy George Sugarman; 61 ©The Denver Public Library, Western History Department; 62 ©Malcolm Kirk/Getty Images; 63 ©Cecilia De Torres, Ltd; 64 Courtesy Patricia Walker; 65 Buffalo Bill Historical Center, Cody WY Chandler-Pohrt Collection, Gift of The Searle Family Trust and The Paul Stock Foundation; 66 International Folk Art Foundation Collection. Museum of International Folk Art. Santa Fe, New Mexico. Photo by: Pat Pollard; 67 Complimentary Jane Hudak Collection; 68 ©Peter Pearson/Stone/Getty Images, Inc; 69 Collection American Folk Art. New York, New York. Gift of Mr. and Mrs. William B. Wigton 1984.25.12. Photo by Schecter Lee; 70 Collection of Nan Yoshida; 71 Museum of International Folk Art. Santa Fe, New Mexico; 72 International Folk Art Foundation Collection. Museum of International Folk Art. Santa Fe, New Mexico. Photo by: Pat Pollard; 73 Smithsonian National Museum of the American Indian, New York; 74 Photograph © Frank Fortune; 75 Virginia Museum of Fine Arts, Richmond. The Arthur and Margaret Glasgow Fund. Katherine Wetzel, photographer; 76 The Brooklyn Museum, Brooklyn, New York; 77 Cranbrook Institute of Science. Photo ©1992 The Detroit Institute of Arts; 78 The Metropolitan Museum of Art. New York, New York; 79 Kimbell Museum of Art; 80 Founders Society Purchase with fund from Flint Ink Corporation. Photo ©1988 The Detroit Institute of Arts; 81 Museum of Fine Arts. Boston, MA; 82 ©Dwell Magazine; 83 ©Natural History Museum, Bucharest, Romania/ Art Resource, NY; 84 San Antonio Museum of Art.

SRAonline.com

Copyright © 2005 by SRA/McGraw-Hill.

All rights reserved. Except as permitted under the United States Copyright Act, no part of this publication may be reproduced or distributed in any form or by any means, or stored in a database or retrieval system, without the prior written permission of the publisher, unless otherwise indicated.

Send all inquiries to:
SRA/McGraw-Hill
4400 Easton Commons
Columbus, OH 43219

Printed in the United States of America.

ISBN 0-07-601834-2

2 3 4 5 6 7 8 9 DBH 08 07

Table of Contents

Begay, Harrison 3
Benton, Thomas Hart 4
Berry, Martha 5
Bishop, Isabel 6
Bonnard, Pierre 7
Butterfield, Deborah 8
Calder, Alexander 9
Cassatt, Mary 10
Cézanne, Paul 11
Chagall, Marc 12
Copley, John Singleton 13
da Vinci, Leonardo 14
Davis, Stuart 15
Dürer, Albrecht 16
Eyre, Ivan 17
Fish, Janet 18
Fonseca, Harry 19
Garza, Carmen Lomas 20
Gile, Selden Connor 21
Harris, Lawren S. 22
Hartigan, Grace 23
Hepworth, Barbara 24
Herbin, Auguste 25
Hockney, David 26
Hofmann, Hans 27
Homer, Winslow 28
Johns, Jasper 29
Jones, Loïs Mailou 30
Kahn, Wolf 31
Kandinsky, Wassily 32
Kelly, Ellsworth 33
Kohlmeyer, Ida 34
Lawrence, Jacob 35
Lazzell, Blanche 36
Liu, Hung 37
Lipchitz, Jacques 38
Magritte, René 39
Mangold, Sylvia Plimack 40
Marquet, Albert 41
Matisse, Henri 42

Mc Intosh, Harrison 43
Mondrian, Piet 44
Moore, Henry 45
Moroles, Jesús 46
Münter, Gabriele 47
Norman, Joseph 48
O'Keeffe, Georgia 49
Oldenburg, Claes 50
Picasso, Pablo 51
Prendergast, Maurice 52
Puruntatameri, Francesca 53
Rousseau, Henri 54
Ruiz, Antonio 55
Schapiro, Miriam 56
Seaweed, Joe 57
Snowden, Gilda 58
Stella, Frank 59
Sugarman, George 60
Tait, Agnes 61
Tamayo, Rufino 62
Torres García, Joaquín 63
Walker, Patricia 64
Arapaho Man's shirt 65
Bridal Bed Cover 66
Chinese Children's Slippers 67
Corn Palace 68
Four Patch in Triangles Quilt 69
Hmong Story Cloth 70
Kente Cloth 71
Letter Holder or Book Cover 72
Man's Headband of Toucan Feathers 73
Mola 74
Ngady Mask 75
Plaque 76
Potawatomi Turban 77
Ritual Figure 78
Seated Arhat 79
Sioux Moccasins 80
Standing Youth 81
The Dwell House 82
The Thinker 83
Tortilla Molds 84

Harrison Begay
1917-2003

Harrison Begay (hâr´ is sən be gā´) was born in White Cone, Arizona. A member of the Navajo tribe, he and his family lived in a hogan and herded sheep and goats for a living. His family found or raised most of what they needed on their own land because the trading post was a long way from their home. Begay studied art under Dorothy Dunn at the Santa Fe Indian School before attending Black Mountain College in North Carolina and Phoenix Junior College in Arizona. He also served three years in the army. Begay began exhibiting his paintings, watercolors, and silkscreens in 1946. He is most famous for his renditions of horses and deer, which were among his favorite subjects. His works are included in such noted museum collections as the Smithsonian Institute, the Museum of Modern Art in New York, and the Museum of the American Indian. Begay won numerous awards for his work, including the French Palmes d'Academique in 1945.

About Art History

Begay's designs were suitable for serigraphy, and this made his work affordable. In 1951 in Santa Fe, Begay was a founder of Tewa Enterprises, one of the few publishing houses to promote Native American Art. American Indian artists including Allan Houser, Frank Vigil, Pop Chalee, and Gerald Nailor sold reproductions through Tewa Enterprises.

About the Artwork

Begay often depicted animals, including antelope, deer, sheep, and horses, as well as lively scenes of Navajos interacting with the environment. He also focused on weaving looms as subjects. His painting *Two Weavers,* completed in 1946, is such a work. Begay illustrated Ann Crowell's *A Hogan for the Bluebird,* published in 1969, which is a story of a Navajo Indian girl who finds it difficult to readjust to the ways of her people after several years at a mission school.

About the Media

Begay preferred to work in watercolors, particularly casein paints.

About the Technique

Begay's palette was often a range of muted pastels. He continued to paint in the style that he helped popularize in the 1930s. His style was at once decorative and lifelike, and his color was clear in hue and even in value. The Navajo conception of the balance of forces is evidenced in Begay's style, which is somehow still but undeniably active.

Artist Profile

Thomas Hart Benton
1889-1975

Thomas Hart Benton (tom´ əs hart bent´ ən) was a regional American painter known for his energetic, colorful murals. He was the son of a United States congressional representative and named after his great uncle, a famous pre-American Civil War senator. From his family, Benton developed a strong identity as an American. He studied art in Paris and at the Art Institute of Chicago. Benton believed that American artists should develop their own styles and not just copy French painting styles. Although Benton began his art career as a cartoonist, he was known for his murals depicting scenes from the rural past of the American Midwest.

About Art History

Benton painted subjects from mostly one region—the American Midwest. He helped develop and promote the American art style known as *regionalism*. He urged American artists to paint scenes from the lives of ordinary Americans. He also encouraged his students to try new ideas in their work. One of his students was the famous painter Jackson Pollock.

About the Artwork

Benton enjoyed painting Midwestern farm scenes. Many of his paintings show sunburned farmers and huge work horses. In *Cradling Wheat,* several farmers and one of their sons are shown harvesting wheat by hand. Benton's paintings remind viewers of days gone by in rural America.

About the Media

Along with other media, Benton used oil and egg tempera.

About the Technique

Benton used his experience as a cartoonist in his later paintings by dividing scenes with borders, like a comic strip.

Artist Profile

Martha Berry
b. 1948

Cherokee beadwork artist Martha Berry (mär´ thə bâr´ rē) was born and raised in Oklahoma by parents of Cherokee, English, and Scotch-Irish descent. At the age of five, her mother and grandmother taught her how to sew, and by the time she was nine she was making her own clothes. When Berry was 20, she worked as a seamstress for a touring ice show. She did not explore her Cherokee heritage until she was in her forties. In only six years Berry became an award-winning beadwork artist. She has displayed her work in many exhibitions and museums.

About Art History

Berry began her beadwork career by creating plains-style designs, but didn't start doing Cherokee beadwork until the principal chief of the Cherokee Nation, Chad Smith, encouraged her to study it. She wrote to numerous art museums requesting photos of Cherokee beadwork and received many to study. Berry also received a grant that enabled her to study the pre-1850 Southeastern Woodlands beadwork in the Smithsonian Institution collection. This opportunity influenced her choice of stitch technique, fabric color, and bead color.

About the Artwork

Berry's beadwork is inspired by the styles of the Southeastern Woodland Native Americans including Cherokee, Chickasaw, Choctaw, Seminole, and other nations. Her many creations include bandolier bags, moccasins, baldrics, and belts, each with different symbols and patterns. Her beaded bandolier bag, *Dance by Numbers,* was inspired by Cherokee number and color symbolism, with emphasis on the numbers two, four, and seven. These numbers are important in Cherokee lore and ceremony, and the beaded seven-point star represents the seven clans being called to dance counterclockwise around the central fire. The two rows of beaded trim symbolize the importance of maintaining balance in life.

About the Media

The glass beads used in Berry's beadwork range in size but are usually quite small. They are sewn closely together to create the impression of continuous lines or fields of color.

About the Technique

Berry researched Cherokee beadwork, and she uses traditional styles combined with her own designs to express the stories and lore of her heritage. Drawn patterns help her measure and sketch the coordinates for her beads. It takes a long time to stitch each design, because each bead is sewn carefully to the cloth background with geometric precision.

Artist Profile

Isabel Bishop
1902–1988

Isabel Bishop (iz´ a bel bish´ əp) was born in Cincinnati, Ohio. A year later, her family moved to a run-down neighborhood in Detroit, Michigan, where her father was employed as the principal of a nearby high school. Her parents didn't think the neighborhood children made good playmates, so Bishop spent much of her time alone. She graduated from high school at age 15 and then studied art. She moved to New York City, where she continued to study art and began exhibiting her work. She loved to paint the people in Union Square.

Bishop married in 1934, moved to the suburbs, and had a son. She commuted to her studio on the Square every day for 40 years. Looking down from her studio in an office building, she watched the people below as she worked. During her life, Bishop won many awards and honors. Her paintings hang in museums across the nation.

About Art History

Bishop's style was influenced by the Baroque period and especially the work of Peter Paul Rubens. She liked the way he used layers of washes as an underpainting and then added glazes over the painting to create a sense of movement. Bishop's early work was "real beyond reality." It gradually gained an abstract cubist quality as she began to emphasize the patterns she saw in the architecture, colors, and shadows of Union Square.

About the Artwork

Bishop created paintings, drawings, and prints. She is best known for her pictures of Union Square, such as *On the Street*. Sometimes called an "urban realist," she painted the shoppers and workers in the square.

About the Media

Bishop painted in oils over tempera and created etchings in aquatint.

About the Technique

Toward the end of her career, Bishop added transparent veils of color and networks of dots and lines to her paintings. She portrayed people as nearly transparent; they seemed to be moving in a mist, contributing to the overall abstract quality.

Artist Profile

Pierre Bonnard
1867–1947

Pierre Bonnard (pyâr bô när´) was born at Fontenay-aux-Roses, a suburb of Paris, France. Although Bonnard studied law, he spent his free time painting at Académie Julien and the École des Beaux-Arts. Eventually he left law altogether and, after joining with a group of experimental artists, exhibited his paintings throughout France, Europe, and the United States. Despite his fame Bonnard was a quiet, private man.

About Art History

Bonnard and other artists from the Académie Julien formed a group called the *Nabis,* or prophets. The Nabis were influenced by *impressionism,* a down-to-earth spontaneous painting style, and *symbolism,* a style using symbols and strong colors. The core of the Nabis included artists such as Edouard Vuillard and Maurice Denis and had an important effect upon graphic art and design. Bonnard became friends with other artists, such as Henri de Toulouse-Lautrec, a post-impressionist artist. When the group separated in 1900, Bonnard developed his own, emotionally charged style. Although at first many people did not like this new style, Bonnard's work became popular after 1920.

About the Artwork

Bonnard painted cheerful landscapes, small genre works and portraits. He used his wife as a model for more than 300 paintings. He also created designs for objects such as pottery, fans, stained glass, and furniture. Toward the end of his life Bonnard created more abstract paintings and focused on the use of color and light.

About the Media

Bonnard worked in a variety of media. He created paintings, lithographs, posters, sculptures, book illustrations, and designs for many common objects.

About the Technique

Through the use of bright colors and strong brushstrokes, Bonnard created expressive, emotionally rich paintings. In his paintings, light seems to transform people, objects, and colors.

Artist Profile

Deborah Butterfield
b. 1949

Deborah Butterfield (deb´ ə rä but´ tər fēld) was born in San Diego, California, on the 75th anniversary of the Kentucky Derby. She thought about becoming a veterinarian, but decided to study art instead and received her graduate degree in fine arts from the University of California at Davis. In 1976 she moved to Bozeman, Montana. Butterfield lives on a ranch and trains horses for competition. Her love of horses translates into her sculptures; horses have been her sole subject for many years.

About Art History

Butterfield was influenced by artists such as William T. Wiley, a painter who believed art does not need to be translated into meaning, and Robert Arneson, a ceramicist who challenged the belief that sculpture is not high art. She works in the twentieth-century tradition of assemblage sculpture.

About the Artwork

In the early 1970s Butterfield began creating realistic horse sculptures in plaster. She began using mud and sticks, but by the 1980s she was creating assemblage sculptures using found objects. Her sculptures show her close relationship with and understanding of horses. Butterfield said of her sculptures, "Every one is different. It's like dancing with a new partner. I don't think I'll ever get tired of dancing, you know. I hope I'll be able to dance until I die."

About the Media

The sculptures for which Butterfield is most famous are made from found objects, such as driftwood, automobile parts, and metal junkyard scraps.

About the Technique

When creating her sculptures, Butterfield reshapes the scrap-metal pieces through welding, cutting, and hammering.

Artist Profile

Alexander Calder
1898–1976

Alexander Calder (a leg zan´ dər kôl´ dər) had a mother who painted, and both his father and grandfather were sculptors. Calder liked to make gadgets. He trained to be an engineer. Later he attended art school and worked as a commercial artist. In 1926, he moved to Paris, France, and began to experiment with making tiny circuses out of wood, cork, and wire. In 1931, he used his training as an engineer to create motor-driven sculptures. A year later he invented *mobiles*—sculptures that move in the wind.

Calder traveled to Europe, South America, and Asia with his wife and two daughters. He created works of art wherever he went. His work became very popular. It has appeared in many public buildings, including the Lincoln Center for the Performing Arts in New York City. He never named his work until it was installed. His last mobile, which remains untitled, hangs in the National Gallery of Art in Washington, D.C.

About Art History

Calder was the first artist known for creating mobiles. He also produced what he called *stabiles*. These sculptures look like mobiles, but do not move. Calder sometimes combined mobiles with stabiles. Much of Calder's work is abstract. For example, his sculpture *Hanging Spider* suggests a spider, but does not have eight legs. Calder's style was influenced by his friendship with the surrealist painters Joan Miró and Piet Mondrian.

About the Artwork

Calder meant for his sculptures to suggest movements and shapes from nature, such as clouds, leaves, or waves. Some of his works are very large. For example, a wire sculpture of a woman, *Spring*, is seven feet high.

About the Media

Calder created his mobiles and stabiles from wire and metal, balancing them carefully so they move in the slightest breeze. He also made drawings, paintings, prints, and stage sets.

About the Technique

Calder usually began a large sculpture by first creating a small-scale model. Then he directed the making of the final sculpture.

Artist Profile

Mary Cassatt
1844–1926

Mary Cassatt (mer´ ē kə sat´) was born into an upper middle-class family in western Pennsylvania in 1844. She was enrolled at the Pennsylvania Academy of the Fine Arts from 1861 to 1865. She later studied in Paris, France, in the studios of Géróme and Couture. In 1874, she settled permanently in Paris, where she regularly submitted work to the yearly Salon exhibitions. The painter and sculptor Edgar Degas saw her work at the Salon and invited Cassatt to join the Impressionists in 1887. She was the only American ever to exhibit in the group's shows. During her lifetime, Cassatt's work was more popular in Europe than in the United States. In her spare time, she loved to entertain friends and ride her horses. As Cassatt got older her eyesight began to fail, and by 1914 she was unable to paint.

About Art History

An etching revival in France in 1862 was marked by the founding of the Societe des Aquafortistes (Society of Etchers). The leaders of this revival, Félix Bracquemond and Alfred Cadart, encouraged important painters of the day to make prints. Degas, Manet, Pissarro, and Cassatt were among those who made prints and experimented with graphic techniques.

About the Artwork

Cassatt is famous for painting mothers with their children, though she had no children of her own. Degas reportedly encouraged Cassatt to paint women and children. At the time few artists did so, except in religious scenes. Cassatt also painted quiet moments in the lives of women.

About the Media

Cassatt painted with oils. She also made many pastel and pencil drawings, as well as prints.

About the Technique

Cassatt mixed her colors directly on the canvas. Her compositions were strongly influenced by the asymmetrical arrangements of Japanese wood-block prints.

Artist Profile

Paul Cézanne
1839–1906

Paul Cézanne (paul sā zan´) was born in the south of France in Aix-en-Provence. He is often called the father of modern art. He loved to paint, but people did not like his work much—at least not during his lifetime. He had to beg gallery owners to show his work, and therefore he did not sell many paintings. He inherited money from his parents to pay his bills and buy his paints. He continued painting until a week before he died.

▲ **Paul Cézanne.** (French). *Self Portrait with Hat.*
c. 1879

Oil on canvas. $44\frac{1}{2}$ × 33 inches (113 × 84 cm.)
Kunstmuseum, Bern, Switzerland.

About Art History

Cézanne was a postimpressionist. He was greatly influenced by the painter Camille Pissarro. Pissarro introduced Cézanne to the new impressionist technique for capturing outdoor light. Cézanne combined impressionism with a formal instruction the impressionists had abandoned. He looked closely at things to find their basic forms and shapes. Cézanne painted cylinders, spheres, and cones to show these forms. Sometimes he changed the shapes he saw in nature to make his paintings more interesting. Picasso, Matisse, and other artists studied Cézanne's ideas.

About the Artwork

Cézanne painted landscapes, still lifes, and portraits. Many of his landscapes were of the countryside and mountains near his home. He developed a unique way of representing nature and objects in a highly creative and abstract fashion. Cézanne painted slowly, often taking several days to create a still life. One friend posed 115 times so Cézanne could finish his portrait.

About the Media

Cézanne worked in both oils and watercolors.

About the Technique

Cézanne used bright colors and bold brushstrokes, especially in the skies of his landscapes. He applied the paint in vertical and horizontal lines. He knew that cool colors seem to pull back and warm colors seem to go forward. Cézanne also used different shades of the same color to add shape to his subjects. His knowledge made his paintings seem three-dimensional.

Marc Chagall
1887–1985

Marc Chagall (mark sha gäl´) was born in a small town in Russia, Vitebsk, which is now part of Belarus. He studied art in Saint Petersburg and then in Paris, France. After the Russian revolution he served as the director of the art academy in his hometown. From 1919 to 1922, Chagall was the art director of the Moscow Jewish State Theater. He painted murals in the theater lobby and created sets for the shows. In 1923, he moved to France. He spent most of the rest of his life there, except for a brief period of residence in the United States from 1941 to 1948.

About Art History

Chagall was one of the first people to paint pictures that looked like dreams. For example, he created many paintings of animals and people flying through the air, sometimes upside down. Chagall is sometimes referred to as an early surrealist because of his dreamlike style and the element of fantasy in his work.

About the Artwork

Born into a very religious Jewish family, Chagall's work shows the strong influence of his home and his heritage. He included childhood memories and religious images in his work. His work combines memories with folklore and fantasy. Chagall created 12 stained-glass windows for the Hadassah Hospital in Jerusalem, Israel, illustrating the Old Testament. He created canvas murals for the ceiling of the Opera in Paris, in addition to two large canvas murals for the lobby of the Metropolitan Opera House in New York City.

About the Media

Chagall usually worked in oils on canvas. He also created stained-glass windows, and designed costumes for ballet dancers.

About the Technique

Chagall often remembered things from his childhood and drew them on canvas. He covered whole canvases with many pictures of different sizes. He sometimes drew people with just one big eye or animals that looked like monsters. He painted them in bright colors, such as red, blue, and yellow.

UNIT 6 • Lesson 3

John Singleton Copley
1738–1815

John Singleton Copley (jän sing´ gəl tən kä´ plē) was born in Boston one year after his parents arrived from Ireland. His father died, and his mother supported the family by running a tobacco shop. When Copley was 11, his mother married Peter Pelham, who was a printmaker, a painter, and a teacher. Pelham quickly saw young Copley's talent and gave him his first art lessons. Copley also learned from studying prints of paintings by Michelangelo, Raphael, and Rubens. In 1774, he was encouraged to go to Europe to study. He left his family in Boston and toured Europe. His father-in-law was one of the importers of the famous shipment of tea that was dumped in Boston Harbor. Because of that incident, his father-in-law left the Colonies in anger, taking Copley's wife and children with him to London. Copley also went to London, where he enjoyed brief success.

About Art History
Copley was one of the finest American artists of colonial times. In his early paintings, Copley wanted to show people as they were. His paintings were said to be "more real than real." After he moved to England, his work was influenced by British and other European painters. It lost some of its energy and realism.

About the Artwork
Among Copley's early portraits were those of such American patriots as Paul Revere and John Hancock. He also painted English patriots who opposed America's independence. After moving to England, Copley began painting dramatic historical events.

About the Media
Copley worked primarily in oils.

About the Technique
Copley brought life to his early paintings by including objects used by his subjects in their daily lives. He was especially skillful at depicting his subjects' eyes. Through their eyes, he tried to show their characters. At first his art was appreciated and earned high prices. But he was not used to painting a portrait in one five hour session, as was the custom in London, and he soon fell out of fashion. His life ended on a sad note; he was in debt and lonely for his life in America.

▲ **Leonardo da Vinci.** (Italian). *Self-Portrait.* c. 1512
Red chalk. $13\frac{1}{8} \times 8\frac{3}{8}$ inches (33.3 × 21.3 cm.). Royal Library, Turin, Italy.

Artist Profile

Leonardo da Vinci
1452–1519

Leonardo (lē ə när′ dō də vin′ chē) was born in 1452, in the small Tuscan town of Vinci. He was the son of a wealthy Florentine notary and a peasant woman. Even when he was a child, people noticed that he had remarkable abilities. He had gracious manners, a fine sense of humor, great strength, and a curiosity that drove him to explore everything. In the mid-1460s, the family settled in Florence, Italy, where Leonardo was given the best available education. He was apprenticed to Verrocchio as a studio boy in 1466. By 1478, he was recognized as an independent master painter.

About Art History

Leonardo's work is considered the high point of Renaissance art. Leonardo was a genius whose achievements spread into many fields. The young Leonardo wrote, "It is easy to become a universal man," and so he did. He was an engineer, architect, inventor, physician, musician, and astronomer. His designs for the helicopter, tank, and other inventions have been constructed and powered by modern engineers. He wrote everything in mirror writing, a way of writing backwards that can be read by viewing the reflection in a mirror.

About the Artwork

One of Leonardo's most famous works is the *Mona Lisa,* which he carried with him on trips. Another is *The Last Supper,* which took him three years to complete.

About the Media

Leonardo painted in oils, tempera, and a mixture of the two. Some of his experimental paint combinations caused his artwork to flake away. He also worked in sculpture, and designed costumes and play sets.

About the Technique

Leonardo used shadows to make his subjects look three-dimensional. He blurred backgrounds and created aerial perspective.

Artist Profile

Stuart Davis
1894–1964

Stuart Davis (stū´ ərt dā´ vəs) was born in Philadelphia. He left high school when he was only 16 years old and went to New York City to study art. His long career began when he showed some paintings in the Armory Show in New York City in 1913. This large and important show introduced modern art to many Americans. Afterward Davis's career took off. By the 1920s, he was studying cubism. Through the 1940s, many of his paintings showed his love of jazz music. He even gave some of his paintings musical titles.

About Art History

Cubism is a style of art first developed by Pablo Picasso and Georges Braque in the early 1900s. The cubists simplified forms into basic geometric shapes. This style influenced Davis, and he, too, simplified objects into flat-looking, colored shapes.

About the Artwork

Davis was interested in city scenes with many people and factories. He painted pictures of streets in Manhattan and Paris using colorful, geometric shapes. He also painted dense canvases full of many abstract forms. Sometimes he reworked the same picture several times to explore different ways of arranging and coloring the shapes. Often his unusual signature is part of the composition.

About the Media

Davis generally worked in oils on canvas.

About the Technique

Davis began by making many drawings of what he was going to paint. Each time, he simplified the shape. After drawing the shapes on the canvas, he painted them in bright, solid colors.

▲ **Albrecht Dürer.** (German). *Self-Portrait.* 1498.
Oil on panel. $20\frac{1}{2} \times 16\frac{1}{8}$ inches (52×41 cm.).
Museo Nacional del Prado, Madrid, Spain.

Artist Profile

Albrecht Dürer
1471–1528

Albrecht Dürer (al brekt´ dū´ ər) was born in Nuremberg, Germany, in 1471. He was the second son in a family of 18 children. His father was a goldsmith, and it was assumed that he would follow in the family tradition. Because Dürer displayed such skill in drawing, his father apprenticed him to a local painter when he was 15. He married and traveled to Italy when he was 23. In Italy he was introduced to the Renaissance ideal of the artist as an intellectual. He brought this philosophy back to Nuremberg, and set about educating himself in all fields of learning associated with this new approach to art. He studied and wrote about geometry, perspective, proportion, and the nature of art. He also wrote many letters and kept a diary. He was observant, imaginative, energetic, and popular. Many political and religious leaders of this turbulent period were Dürer's friends.

About Art History

Dürer is one of the most famous artists in German history. He was known for his paintings, drawings, prints, and theoretical writings on art. He incorporated the art of Renaissance Italy into the gothic traditions of his country. He had a strong influence on his contemporaries.

About the Artwork

Like other artists of his time, Dürer painted many religious scenes. He often placed small animals in his paintings. For example, his *Adam and Eve* included a cat, an elk, a rabbit, an ox, and other animals. His images of animals and nature were so detailed and realistic that they could have been used in textbooks. Dürer also excelled at portrait painting, and he painted many self-portraits. He had a technical mastery of printmaking as well.

About the Media

Dürer painted with watercolors on paper and oils on wood and canvas. He made many drawings using charcoal and chalk, and produced prints done with engraving and woodcut techniques.

About the Technique

Dürer's training as an engraver and designer of woodcuts gave him excellent drawing skills. His portraits show the hearts and souls of his subjects, as well as an accurate likeness. He painted so smoothly that no brushstrokes are visible.

Artist Profile

Ivan Eyre
b. 1935

Ivan Eyre (ī´ vən ēr) was born in rural Saskatchewan, a province in Canada. His family was extremely poor. They moved from place to place throughout Canada as his father looked for work. When Eyre was in fifth grade, he won a prize for painting. His teachers encouraged him to continue making art. He went to after-school art classes while he was in high school. After he graduated, he went to art school in Winnipeg. In 1967, the Canada Council paid for him to travel around Europe. He returned from his travels to teach in Winnipeg, Manitoba. He has also taught art at the University of North Dakota and the University of Manitoba.

About Art History

Ivan Eyre is an individualist in the art world. He does not belong to or work with any groups of artists. Eyre's work is difficult to categorize, because he often crosses boundaries of styles, themes, and media.

About the Artwork

In his artwork, Eyre tries to show how poverty and misery can be overcome with happy situations. Although Eyre has lived through wars, car accidents, and natural disasters, he wants to show that he has experienced more than this pain and anxiety. Most of his paintings combine elements of nature with those of civilization. Distorted figures that are long, angular, and unrealistically flat appear in many of his paintings. He paints many landscapes of wooded forests. Some of these appear to be seen through frames, as if the viewer is looking out a window. Sharp protrusions poke out of the frame toward the viewer.

About the Media

Eyre paints with acrylics and oils on canvas.

About the Technique

Eyre paints strong, heavy lines around his figures, which seem to float on his canvases. He uses analogous colors, usually all from one color family. The landscapes he paints show wide angles, often from above. His still lifes are set at unusual angles. They are often framed by a windowsill or an imaginary, unusually shaped frame. Sometimes Eyre applies shiny glazes over parts of his acrylic paintings to accent those areas.

Janet Fish
b. 1938

Janet Fish (jan´ ət fish) earned two degrees in fine arts from Yale University but struggled to find work. For a while, she supported herself by painting bars of soap for a department store. Since then her large, lively still lifes have become much admired. Fish has taught at art schools across the nation. She now spends half her time in New York and half in Vermont.

About Art History
During the 1960s, Fish was part of a group of nontraditional painters. She is known as a realistic painter, but much of her work incorporates abstract qualities. For example, she might exaggerate the shapes of bottles and repeat those shapes within a painting.

About the Artwork
Fish's still lifes, landscapes, and portraits make ordinary objects seem extraordinary. She might begin painting a bottle of window cleaner or gummy candy, which she uses to create a fascinating combination of colors, contrasting surfaces, and light. She is especially interested in the effects of light, such as how it shines through a crystal bowl or on cut flowers.

About the Media
Fish's work includes both oil and watercolor paintings.

About the Technique
Fish carefully chooses and arranges the objects in her still lifes. She tries to feel a connection to the objects and to understand how the objects relate to one another. She is concerned about color, texture, and balance in her paintings. To increase the impact of her work she often paints objects three or four times larger than they really are. They usually fill the picture, crowding right up to the edge. Fish aims to paint still lifes that do not hold still.

Artist Profile

Harry Fonseca
b. 1946

Harry Fonseca (har´ ē fōn´ sā´ kə) was born in California to parents of Maidu, Hawaiian, and Portuguese heritage. The Maidu tribe is a gatherer tribe of central California, and Harry grew up appreciating the culture's use of rich color and design. He also grew up with few books and little exposure to art, but he studied art in college in Sacramento. Fonseca's parents did not understand why he chose to pursue painting and thought it impractical, but he continued to successfully explore his own independent style and method despite the skepticism of others.

About Art History

In college, Fonseca was interested in the art of Latin America, Africa, and the South Pacific. When he visited a painted rock cave in Sacramento, he discovered *petroglyphs*, which are ancient pictures carved onto rocks and cave walls. Fonseca appreciates the mythology of his heritage along with that of many other native peoples. In order to keep in contact with this rich culture, the artist lives and works in Santa Fe, New Mexico.

About the Artwork

Fonseca was inspired by the playfulness and linear quality of the petroglyphs he saw in Sacramento and admired their color and designs. Much of his work utilizes this playfulness, especially his *Coyote* series that highlights the trickster nature of the coyote. Fonseca sometimes depicts the coyote in human clothing and contemporary environments, as seen in his piece *Coyote Koshari*. This series also refers to religions that recognize the coyote as both creator and destroyer, addressing the serious attributes of its sacred nature. Fonseca has also used his painting as a way to explore social justice concerns and his veneration for certain religious figures such as Saint Francis.

About the Media

One of the artist's series, *Stone Poems,* was created with many yards of canvas painted with house-paint brushes. Fonseca uses both stretched and unstretched canvas for his mixed-media creations.

About the Technique

In order to mimic the appearance of petroglyphs, Fonseca makes sketches of the actual stone carvings and then bases his paintings and creations on those sketches.

Artist Profile

Carmen Lomas Garza
b. 1948

Carmen Lomas Garza (kär´ mān lō´ mäs gär´ sä) was born in Kingsville, Texas. She grew up in a Hispanic home where both Spanish and English were spoken. When she and her brother started school, many of their classmates made fun of them for speaking English with an accent. Garza often felt that she did not fit in. This feeling led her to develop stronger ties with her family and community. She decided she wanted to be an artist when she was only 13 years old. She studied art at the Texas Arts and Industry University and earned a master's degree from San Francisco State University.

About Art History
Garza is a major contemporary Hispanic artist. Her aim is to produce works of art that show the beauty of Hispanic culture. She incorporates Hispanic art with American culture in her bilingual children's books about families. Her first bilingual book was *Family Pictures/Cuadros de Famila*, published in 1990.

About the Artwork
Garza's paintings tell stories about growing up Hispanic in Texas. She paints many *monitos*, or "little people," paintings. These paintings often portray families dancing, working, preparing food, or eating.

About the Media
Garza paints with oil, acrylic, or gouache paints on canvas or linen. She also makes etchings, paper cutouts, and prints.

About the Technique
Garza often uses rich colors and simple shapes in her paintings.

Artist Profile

Selden Connor Gile
1877–1947

Selden Connor Gile (sel´ dôn con´ nər gīl) was born on a farm in Maine and later went to business college. He moved to California, and sold ceramic building materials before teaching himself to paint. Gile loved the outdoors, was an avid hiker, and was known for being an excellent cook and host. Many artists sought his good-natured company, and it was through his warm hospitality and energy that the Society of Six was formed in the 1920s.

About Art History

Along with Maurice Logan, William Clapp, Bernard von Eichman, August Gay, and Louis Siegriest, Gile formed the *Society of Six,* artists who incorporated impressionism and fauvism into sunny Oakland, California landscapes in the 1920s. Gile shared his house with many aspiring artists, and was renowned for his genial company and vibrant hosting. He had a wide circle of creative friends. He exhibited with The Six in the Oakland Art Gallery, and did some traveling in America's Southwest. In 1927, Gile moved north of Oakland and continued to paint, although he became friends with a heavy-drinking crowd that negatively affected his work. Gile's career came to an end in 1947, when he died of complications related to his alcohol consumption.

About the Artwork

Gile's passion for outdoor activity fostered momentum for his painting, and almost all of his subject matter consisted of brightly colored landscapes, including the painting *Two Fishermen and a Boat.* His use of bright color throughout his 30 years of painting is similar to that of the French fauves. His expressive brushwork and brightly lit scenes mirrored his genuine enthusiasm and physical energy, both of which were unique to the California painting culture.

About the Media

Gile worked primarily in oil paints on panel and canvas and promoted the use of lively colors. Bright sunlight was often included in his work, and many of his paintings were created with a warm palette.

About the Technique

Gile would hike through the hills of California to locate a potential setting, and then would set up his materials. In this way his depictions of light and nature were captured and painted directly from their original source. Gile's energetic brushstrokes allowed him freedom from conventional realism, and produced a modern spin on realistic representation.

Artist Profile

Lawren S. Harris
1885–1970

Lawren Harris (lôr´ ən hâr´ is) came from a wealthy Canadian family. He was in college when a math professor noticed his pencil drawings. The professor talked Harris's mother into sending him to art school. After studying art in Germany, Harris began his career by illustrating magazine articles. In 1908, on a trip for a magazine, Harris saw his first winter in the Canadian wilderness. He showed that winter beauty in his realistic art. By the time Harris married in 1910 he was already selling his paintings. In 1930 he took a dangerous two-month cruise on a Canadian supply ship into the frozen Arctic. Afterward he painted many scenes from that vast wilderness. After a divorce and remarriage, Harris shifted to abstract art. Then he created his favorite winter landscapes with triangles and spheres.

About Art History

Harris and six other Canadian painters, including Tom Thomson, formed an organization called the Group of Seven. The painters helped promote their nation's artists. Harris liked to try new styles and paint different things. He is known as a regionalist painter, and is one of Canada's most important artists.

About the Artwork

Harris loved winter landscapes. He especially loved the beauty of snow-topped fir trees. His paintings often showed the northern lights on fields of snow and ice. He also drew poor urban neighborhoods, but he seemed more interested in the buildings than in the people who lived there.

About the Media

Harris used pencil, charcoal, watercolors, and oils.

About the Technique

Harris most often used soft, muted colors, such as mauve, pink, pale blue, and cream. Many of his urban scenes include strong horizontal and vertical lines that give structure to the paintings. In his landscapes, strong brushstrokes show the rugged land.

Artist Profile

Grace Hartigan
b. 1922

Grace Hartigan (grās härt´ ti gən) began her career in the 1950s as one of the most promising young abstract expressionist painters in New York. A member of the second generation of artists to work in the new style, Hartigan distinguished herself early on. Her art was chosen for important gallery and museum exhibitions, and she was hailed as a rising art star in national magazines such as *Life* and *Fortune*. For the first years of her career, she was known as George Hartigan, after the female novelists George Sand and George Eliot. Hartigan identified passionately with the liberated lifestyles of these women.

About Art History
In the years just after World War II, the United States became a global power and American artists practicing a new style known as abstract expressionism emerged as leaders in the art world. For the first time, western Europeans began to look to New York for artistic direction. Abstract expressionism uses a nonrepresentational approach to color and form in order to express emotions. Along with Helen Frankenthaler, Joan Mitchell, and Nell Blaine, Hartigan was among the most important practitioners of abstract expressionism in the 1950s. Accepted by their male peers, they were independent women who thought of themselves as artists first, women second.

About the Artwork
Hartigan's large, abstract paintings are made of energetic, spontaneous brushwork with raw, sometimes jarring color. She has said that she wanted to paint like nature—free and uncensored. Hartigan's paintings suggest vivid glimpses of urban and natural landscapes. After 1959, her paintings became more fluid and lyrical and increasingly mystical and symbolic in content.

About the Media
Hartigan paints in oils on canvas.

About the Technique
Hartigan applies large amounts of oil paint to the canvas with a variety of broad and narrow commercial paint brushes. In many areas of the canvas the brushwork is very thick. This is known as *impasto*.

Artist Profile

Barbara Hepworth
1903-1975

Barbara Hepworth (bärb´ ə rə hep´ wûrth) was an English sculptor known for her abstract works in wood, stone, and metal. As a child in Yorkshire, she took car trips through the countryside with her father. She was impressed by the contrast between the beauty of rural areas and the grime of industrial towns. The land became a theme she returned to again and again in her art. After studying art and sculpture in England, Hepworth moved to Rome and then returned to England. She married twice, once to a sculptor and once to a painter. She had a son and a set of triplets. Her relationship with her children also became an important theme of her work. In 1965, she was honored by being named a dame of the British Empire.

About Art History
Hepworth's early work was influenced by the sculpture of Jean Arp and Constantin Brancusi, as well as the artwork of her friend Henry Moore. Hepworth and Moore were the most important English sculptors of their time.

About the Artwork
Hepworth was fascinated by relationships. In her sculpture *Mother and Child,* two figures form a single curved shape, indicating their close bond. She expressed her love of nature in such abstract sculptures as *Wave and Tides II.* Hepworth's rounded forms seem to have been shaped by nature instead of a chisel. These sculptures also show her interest in the relationship between the subject and space. She hollowed out forms or pierced them with holes so the space within the sculpture is as important as the sculpture itself. Hepworth often painted the inside surfaces of her sculptures to emphasize the open spaces. She also defined the openings by stretching strings across them. Some of her sculptures are small enough to hold in one hand. Others tower 20 feet above viewers.

About the Media
Hepworth sculpted in wood, stone, marble, alabaster, slate, copper, and bronze.

About the Technique
Hepworth sketched her sculptures before carving them. For her bronze sculptures, she first made plaster models. Her works are notable for their superb finishes.

Artist Profile

Auguste Herbin
1882–1960

Auguste Herbin (ō gūst´ âr´ ban) was born in France and studied at the École des Beaux-Arts. Later he went to other countries to paint. In Italy, he noticed how different kinds of light changed the way things look. From then on he tried to ignore little details and paint only the main part of his subject. Herbin was enthusiastic and curious and loved his work. During the last years of his life Herbin created tapestry designs.

About Art History

Herbin explored the geometric, cubist style of painting. He made the subjects in his paintings more and more simplistic until they were only outlines or symbols. He was interested in shapes and colors, and studied how different colors make people feel. Herbin also read about optical illusions and used them in some of his paintings. Herbin was a leader of the abstract creation school of art along with Georges Vantongerloo. Abstract creationists wanted to create purely abstract art, reducing their works to the basic elements of color and form. Wassily Kandinsky was another member of this school of painters.

About the Artwork

Early in his career, Herbin painted large still lifes and landscapes. In time his paintings became so symbolic that it was hard to tell what he had painted. His later paintings consisted of geometric shapes rendered in bright colors.

About the Media

Herbin most frequently painted with oils.

About the Technique

Herbin used flat, intense colors and bold shapes. Brushstrokes cannot be detected in Herbin's paintings.

Artist Profile

David Hockney
b. 1937

David Hockney (dā´ vəd häk´ nē) was born in 1937 into a working class family in the northern industrial section of Bradford, England. By the time he was 11, he had decided to become an artist. At 16, he attended the Bradford School of Art, and went on to study at the Royal College of Art. In 1961, he made his first trip to the United States. The brightness and light of California was a sharp contrast from the rain and fog of England. He was impressed by the sense of space in the sprawling city of Los Angeles, and moved permanently to the United States in 1978 to become part of the California art scene.

About Art History

Hockney first made an impact on the art world in the 1960s. He was a leader of the English pop art movement that was centered in London, England. Pop artists were fascinated by how the flood of American mass media was affecting British life. Pop artists used popular or commercial culture as inspiration for their art.

About the Artwork

Hockney is a realistic painter who uses many styles and techniques to tell stories. Much of his artwork relates to his life, family, and friends. Hockney is inspired by the climate and culture of southern California. He is interested in the sunny blue skies and the relaxed lifestyle.

About the Media

Hockney paints with oils and acrylics. He is a stage designer, a printmaker, and a photographer. Hockney creates photo collages that he calls "joiner" photographs. He joins separate photos together to create a unique image that expresses time and movement.

About the Technique

Hockney paints with large areas of bold color. As his style developed he became more interested in how people view his work. He wanted to extend the gaze of his viewers. To create his "joiner" photo collages he alters and combines images to show the passage of time. He may repeat the same image or change the scale or the angle to imply movement. Hockney uses forward and backward progression and organizes all the images to guide the eye to a focal point. He uses an ordinary, automatic 35mm camera and takes a number of pictures in rapid succession.

▲ **Hans Hofmann.** (German/American). *Au Printemps, Springtime.* 1955.

Oil on canvas. 48 × 36 inches (121.92 × 91.44 cm.). Frances Lehman Loeb Art Center, Vassar College, Poughkeepsie, New York.

Artist Profile

Hans Hofmann
1880–1966

Hans Hofmann (hänz hof´man), a German painter, studied art in his homeland and in Paris before opening his own school of modern art in Munich, Germany. As World War II threatened, some of his students who had already moved to New York City arranged a teaching position for him at the Art Students League. Hofmann immigrated to the United States and settled in New York City in 1932. In 1933, he started the Hans Hofmann School of Fine Art. It became one of the most respected art schools in the United States. For 25 years, Hofmann taught art but did little painting of his own. In 1958, he left his school to paint full time. He eventually achieved international recognition.

About Art History

Hofmann's early paintings were expressionistic landscapes and still lifes. He strongly admired the work of the Russian abstract painter Wassily Kandinsky. In time, Hofmann's work became nonobjective. He led the way for painters in the United States to move into abstract expressionism because he influenced so many New York artists. Hofmann also contributed greatly to modern art by focusing on the psychological effects of color and other elements of painting.

About the Artwork

Like other abstract expressionists, Hofmann shared his feelings and ideas in purely abstract images. He used combinations of red, yellow, and green, for example, to express what he called push-pull tension. The reds and yellows push forward, while the greens pull back from the viewer.

About the Media

Hofmann worked mainly in oils.

About the Technique

This artist used brilliant colors, lines that seemed to be moving, and thick layers of paint. In his painting *Flowering Swamp,* for example, two rectangles seem to float over thick layers of color. The combination suggests flowers floating on water.

Artist Profile

Winslow Homer
1836–1910

Winslow Homer (winz´ lō hō´ mər) was born in Boston. He had very little formal training in art, but he showed great artistic talent even in his earliest sketches. He worked as a magazine illustrator for nearly 20 years. When the Civil War began, *Harper's Weekly* sent him to the front lines to sketch both the fighting and ordinary life. Homer did not begin to paint seriously until he was 26. He taught himself the techniques he needed, and eventually settled on the Maine coast. In his later years Homer lived like a hermit, seldom seeing anyone.

About Art History

Homer avoided other artists, other art styles, and art exhibitions. He once said, "If one wishes to become a real artist, one must never look at the work of another artist." His first paintings were very detailed. His later work was simpler and more creative. Homer led American art out of the romanticism of the mid-1800s and into the peak of realism.

About the Artwork

Homer loved nature, especially the sea. Even though he lived in New York City, he never painted city scenes. Instead he painted scenes from nature. Over the years he changed from painting families in farm scenes to painting people struggling with nature, usually the sea. During this period he painted *The Fog Warning*, which shows a man alone in a small boat on a rough sea. Toward the end of his life, Homer stopped putting people in his paintings. Instead, he focused only on nature.

About the Media

Homer is best known for his watercolors, but he also created sketches, wood engravings, and oil paintings. He also worked in charcoal, chalk, and pencil.

About the Technique

Homer was very patient and particular about details. He waited for months for the light to be just right when he was painting *Early Morning at Sea*. He used watercolors in an unusual way for his time. Instead of filling in light areas with white paint, he left the paper white.

UNIT 5 • Lesson 2

Artist Profile

Jasper Johns
b. 1930

Jasper Johns (jas´ pər jänz) was born in Augusta, Georgia. After serving in Japan with the United States Army, he moved to New York City. There he worked in a bookstore and started creating art. When he was 24, he decided to throw away all the art he had ever made. He wanted a fresh start. He was determined to create original art, not copies of the styles of other artists. Since then Johns has been known for his inventiveness.

About Art History

Johns is one of the most important artists in the American pop art movement. Pop artists use everyday objects as the subjects of art. They reject abstract painting styles and techniques like splattering paint on canvases. Pop artists focus on American mass culture, including television, billboard advertising, and cars.

About the Artwork

Much of Johns's artwork shows familiar items such as books, flags, targets, numbers, and maps. He gives an object new meaning by challenging the viewer to look at and study the object rather than use it.

About the Media

Johns varies his media from work to work. In some works he uses a palette knife to apply wax mixed with paint onto the canvas. In other works he uses oil paints. Johns has sculptures cast in bronze.

About the Technique

Early in his career, Johns used precise lines and built up paint in thick layers on his canvases. His later paintings are less exact and more abstract. Johns has also made realistic bronze sculptures of commonplace objects such as coffee cans.

Artist Profile

Loïs Mailou Jones
1905–1998

Loïs Mailou Jones (lō´ is mī´ lü jōnz) had a long, successful career as an artist and received national and international recognition. As a teacher she affected generations of students. Her early studies at the School of the Museum of Fine Arts in Boston, Massachusetts, emphasized design. She also worked as a textile designer. A 1937–1938 fellowship at the Académie Julian in Paris introduced her to European modernism. Between 1930 and 1977, Jones taught art at Howard University in Washington, D.C. In 1953, she married a Haitian artist and began to travel to Haiti. In the late 1960s and early 1970s, she undertook a massive research project at Howard University called "The Black Visual Arts." It was a compilation of slides and biographies of African, Haitian, and African American artists.

About Art History

The styles in which Jones worked range from impressionism to realism to abstraction. In her African-inspired work of the 1970s, she endeavored to explore the unity of all African art by combining motifs from various regions. Geometric patterns of African textiles underlie many of these paintings.

About the Artwork

Jones's subject matter includes African-inspired themes, French landscapes and cityscapes, scenes of Haiti, and themes of social realism. *Esquisse for Ode to Kinshasa* was painted following Jones's 1970 trip to Africa, where she interviewed artists in 11 African nations. She paid tribute to Kinshasa, the capital city of Zaire (now the Democratic Republic of the Congo), in her stylized rendering of an African shield.

About the Media

Jones worked in acrylic, a fast-drying paint in which the pigment is suspended in a clear, plastic medium.

About the Technique

The vibrant colors and the abstract, two-dimensional forms of Jones's work reflect the visual elements she absorbed during her studies in Africa.

UNIT 2 • Overview

Wolf Kahn
b. 1927

Wolf Kahn (woolf kän) was born in Germany to Jewish parents. His mother died when he was five. He lived in Germany with his grandmother for a while. Then he was sent to England in 1939 just before World War II broke out. The next year he traveled to the United States to live with his father. As a young man Kahn studied abstract expressionist painting. Now he has his own approach to art. In the early 1950s, Kahn helped set up an art gallery in New York City. Since then his work has been shown nationwide.

About Art History

Kahn is sometimes called "a school of one." He mixes realism with abstraction to show a style called *abstract expressionism*. Rather than show exactly what he sees, he shows how a scene makes him feel. He uses layers of color and light. Kahn's work is also called *modernist*.

About the Artwork

In his work, Kahn tries to show the shifting light and atmosphere in landscapes. He is interested in the natural difference between sky and land. Kahn often uses more color in the sky and less color in the land.

About the Media

Kahn works in pastels, which he calls "the dust on the butterflies' wings." Pastels are sticks of colored powder mixed with oils, similar to chalk. Kahn likes pastels because they can show sharp contrasts and delicate tints. He believes the dusty quality of the powder adds to the beauty of his work.

About the Technique

Kahn uses glowing violets, oranges, and pinks, along with quiet grays. These give Kahn the hazy images he likes. He adds layers of colors until he gets the effect he wants. Kahn often creates a quick sketch outdoors and then completes it in his studio. He also might paint the same scene in larger or smaller versions.

Artist Profile

Wassily Kandinsky
1866–1944

Wassily Kandinsky (va sēl´ ē kan din´ skē) first tried painting as a teenager in his native Russia. Even then he felt that each color had a mysterious life of its own. He was still drawn to colors and painting while he studied law and economics in college, but he believed that art was "a luxury forbidden to a Russian." In time, he moved to Germany, studied art, and began his career. Throughout his life Kandinsky moved back and forth between Russia and Germany. In 1933 he settled in France after Nazi storm troopers labeled his painting style "degenerate."

About Art History

Kandinsky was a pioneer in the pure abstract painting style—a combination of color and form with no subject matter. He did not give a title to a painting he did in 1910, but others called it the *First Abstract Watercolour.* Kandinsky felt that trying to paint recognizable objects distracted artists from their real jobs of expressing ideas and emotions. He believed communicating through painting was similar to communicating with music. He often gave his paintings titles that were musical and abstract, such as *Improvisation 30.*

About the Artwork

It is possible to identify landscapes and objects in some of Kandinsky's early paintings, but his later work was entirely abstract. Only occasionally during World War I did Kandinsky include cannons and other recognizable objects in his work.

About the Media

Kandinsky worked in oils, watercolors, and India ink.

About the Technique

Kandinsky did not try to show the essence of his subjects because he had none. Instead, he attempted to make forms and colors take on meaning separate from the physical world. His work often impresses even viewers who are not certain what the paintings mean.

Artist Profile

Ellsworth Kelly
b. 1923

Ellsworth Kelly (elz´ wûrth ke´ lē) was born in Newburgh, New York. During high school, he studied art and theatre. After graduation, he could not decide which he wanted to pursue as a career, but he eventually chose art. In 1941, he began to study at the Pratt Institute in Brooklyn, New York. In 1943, he volunteered to serve with the army during World War II, and after the war he went back to his art studies. He studied at the School of the Museum of Fine Arts in Boston, Massachusetts. From 1948 to 1954, he lived in France, studying art and architecture. In 1954, he returned to New York.

About Art History

Kelly integrates painting and sculpture. He experiments with the shapes and sizes of canvases. These experiments led him to explore sculpture and three-dimensional or free-standing art. He is interested in color and shape, and was a leader of the hard-edge color field painting artistic movement, which began during the late 1950s.

About the Artwork

Kelly creates sculptures influenced by the color field painting movement. He uses the same geometric shapes and colors of this painting style. He used painting canvases for his early sculptures. His best-known later works are panel paintings, which consist of several canvases—as many as 64—joined together. Each canvas is painted with a different, intense color.

About the Media

In color field painting, the canvas is stained with thin, translucent color washes. The color washes are made of acrylic, ink, or oil that can be diluted. Mixed with a solvent, the color flows freely.

About the Technique

Kelly wants his work to communicate unexpected effects. He pays great attention to details of color and shape and creates unexpected effects by changing these details. His paintings are often only one color or black and white, and the canvases are different shapes. Placing one painting next to other paintings of similar sizes but different colors creates an unexpected effect. In his sculpture Kelly experiments with the different shapes of objects and how the shapes relate to each other.

• Artist Profile •

Ida Kohlmeyer
1911–1997

▲ **Ida Kohlmeyer.** (American). *Symbols.* 1981.
Oil, graphite, and pastel on canvas.
$69\frac{1}{2} \times 69$ inches (176.53 × 175.26 cm.).
National Museum of Women in the Arts, Washington, D.C.

Ida Kohlmeyer (ī´ də kōl´ mī ûr) grew up Ida Rittenberg in New Orleans, Louisiana. She began her artistic career in her late thirties, after taking art classes in a neighborhood art school. Her talent was quickly recognized, and she was encouraged to continue with formal art training. At 45, she graduated with a master of fine arts degree in painting from Tulane University. Kohlmeyer's early work was primarily figurative, but under the influence of Hans Hofmann at his school in Provincetown, Massachusetts, and Mark Rothko, a visiting artist-in-residence at Tulane University, she moved toward abstraction. A dedicated, prolific artist, Kohlmeyer has paintings and sculptures in many important collections. She is particularly famous in her hometown of New Orleans, where her accomplishments were honored by the city's mayor, who declared March, 1985 "Ida Kohlmeyer Month."

About Art History

Kohlmeyer developed her unique style in the 1970s under the influence of the abstract expressionists Hans Hofmann and Mark Rothko. *Abstract expressionism,* a nonrepresentational style of painting, prevailed among New York School painters in the 1950s. Instead of depicting real objects or people, abstract expressionists used shapes, lines, brushstrokes, and colors to convey ideas or emotions. The canvases are typically bold, dynamic, and large in scale.

About the Artwork

Paintings by Kohlmeyer span several phases of her artistic development. *Symbols* is an example of her cluster compositions in which she organizes pictographs, stylized pictures, or marks into a gridlike pattern. Sometimes these pictographs are recognizable symbols, such as hearts, bells, stars, and apples, and at other times they are spontaneous, calligraphic marks resembling handwriting and doodles.

About the Media

Kohlmeyer used oil paint, graphite, and pastels.

About the Technique

Kohlmeyer applied paint in heavy layers and strokes that she pushed and pulled across the canvas to expose underpainting. Her clusters in a grid formation are sometimes isolated within their own boxes, like a patchwork quilt or checkerboard. Other times, as in *Symbols,* she lets them float freely over the flat background of the canvas. The seeming spontaneity and movement of her marks and symbols are stabilized by their placement in horizontal and vertical rows.

Artist Profile

Jacob Lawrence
1917–2000

Jacob Lawrence (jā´ kəb lär´ ənz) had parents who met on their migration to the North. His father was born in South Carolina, and his mother in Virginia. Lawrence was born in Atlantic City, New Jersey, in 1917. The family finally settled in Harlem in 1929 at the end of the Harlem Renaissance. Because his mother worked all day, she enrolled Lawrence in the Harlem Art Workshop after school to keep him out of trouble. He had many excellent teachers there, including Charles Alston. Lawrence won a scholarship to the American Artists School. He taught at New York's Pratt Institute from 1958 to 1965. From 1970, he taught at the University of Washington in Seattle, where he also served as head of the art department. He won many awards in his lifetime, including the Presidential Medal of Arts.

About Art History

Lawrence's paintings not only contribute to the art world, they also add to our knowledge of African American history. Lawrence painted African American heroes, such as Harriet Tubman and Frederick Douglass.

About the Artwork

Lawrence's most famous work is a series of 60 paintings called *Migration of the Negro*. The paintings tell a story which begins at a train station in the South and ends at a station in the North. The scenes he chose to paint focus on the struggle of leaving one life for another and the search for freedom and dignity. His paintings did not overlook the harshness and violence that was part of this migration. During World War II he served in the U.S. Coast Guard and created a series of paintings about his experiences. They were exhibited by the Museum of Modern Art in 1944.

About the Media

Lawrence painted on paper with *gouache*, an opaque watercolor paint, similar to tempera paint used in schools. It covers the paper with a smooth, matte coat. He was also a printmaker.

About the Technique

Lawrence said a lot about his subjects with only a few lines and carefully chosen colors. He used many neutral colors, such as taupe, mocha, and charcoal, and balanced them with splashes of bright color.

Artist Profile

Blanche Lazzell
1878-1956

Blanche Lazzell (blanch lə zel´) was credited with being one of the first women to introduce modern art to America. Born in Maidsville, West Virginia, she earned several university degrees, which was unusual for a woman of her time. Lazzell was respected for her printmaking skills and for her experimental woodblock techniques, in which she tried new methods with watercolor instead of ink. Her bold colors and angular compositions hint at an impressionistic influence, while highlighting her innovative style of printmaking.

About Art History

In the early 1900s, Lazzell traveled to Paris, France, and grew very interested in cubism. In 1915, she traveled to Cape Cod, Massachusetts, and joined a group of artists known as the Provincetown Printers. The energy and dynamic production of this art colony influenced Lazzell's work tremendously and inspired her to create some of her most famous prints. During the 1920s, Lazzell studied with Fernand Léger, Andre Lhote, and Albert Gleizes, who advocated for cubism and abstraction.

About the Artwork

The Provincetown Printers developed a unique style of woodblock prints inspired by Japanese color woodcuts. Lazzell's work mirrors that influence and displays a combined style of decoration, abstraction, and geometric and cubist tendencies. In *The Monongahela at Morgantown,* Lazzell incorporated a geometric quality into the boldly colored, abstract forms of rooftops and hills. She completed a number of prints in which she portrayed her family life in West Virginia.

About the Media

Lazzell regarded a successful print as one that embraced originality, simplicity, freedom of expression, and sincerity. She often printed abstract images of flowers and the houses and rooftops of Provincetown, Massachusetts.

About the Technique

Instead of the traditional method of making woodcut prints, where a separate block of wood was cut for each color, the Provincetown Printers' new method allowed them to create a multi-colored composition from a single block of wood. Grooves cut into the wood separate different areas of color. Each groove is not inked so when the block is pressed to the paper, a white outline of paper surrounds each colored area of the print. Lazzell created more than 130 blocks from 1916 to the 1950s.

Artist Profile

Hung Liu
b. 1948

Hung Liu (hung lē oō´) was born in Changchun, China. In the year she was born, her father was taken as a political prisoner. She did not see him again until Father's Day, 50 years later. Although she was a stellar student, political events disrupted her education. She finally graduated from Beijing Teacher's College in 1972, and went on to teach art. Liu began giving lessons in art on her weekly television program, *How to Draw and Paint,* which became extremely popular.

About Art History

The photorealistic representations within Liu's artwork are often derived from photos taken by tourists in China around the turn of the century. These photos captured a part of history that included women with bound feet, women who were exploited, and wounded soldiers. Liu also used photos from albums found in the Beijing film archive that were spared from the book burnings of the Cultural Revolution.

About the Artwork

Liu's artwork reflects the traditional art of China. It incorporates symbols and themes from her homeland, such as bowls, birds, Buddha, and lotus blossoms. Her paintings explore the American and Chinese cultures that inseparably comprise her identity.

About the Media

Liu most often works in oils on canvas.

About the Technique

Liu was on a journey to northern China in 1976 during the Tangshan earthquake, which killed more than 240,000 people. This disaster, along with the political persecution she witnessed throughout her youth, provide the inspiration for many of the images she incorporates into her art. Liu became a United States citizen in 1991 and continues to teach studio art at Mills College in Oakland, California. Liu incorporates a technique called *drip painting* in which her thinned oils drip down the canvas.

UNIT 2 • Lesson 3

Artist Profile

Jacques Lipchitz
1891–1973

Jacques Lipchitz (zhäk lēp´shēts) was born in Lithuania and later moved to France. During World War II Lipchitz, who was Jewish, fled Europe to escape the Nazis. He left Paris and came to the United States. In 1952 a fire destroyed everything in his New York art studio, and he had to start all over. In 1957 he became a citizen of the United States.

About Art History

By the 1930s, Lipchitz was known as one of the leading European sculptors. After meeting the Spanish artist Picasso, Lipchitz was influenced by the cubist style. Both expressionism and surrealism influenced his work. Many of Lipchitz's works had political themes. For example, Lipchitz believed it was important to speak out against Nazism in his work. He tried to convey the idea that to create freely, one must fight evil.

About the Artwork

Lipchitz's work reflects many different styles and themes. Some are realistic, while others are abstract. Some sculptures were planned in detail, and others were made quickly, without much planning. Lipchitz became known for bronze sculptures that he called *transparencies.* These sculptures include solid areas and holes. Lipchitz often used biblical and mythological stories to express his anger about Nazism. For example, he showed David and Goliath with the giant wearing a swastika, the emblem of Nazi Germany.

About the Media

Lipchitz created bronze and stone sculptures as well as wooden panels.

About the Technique

Lipchitz sketched an idea first. Then he made a small model from plaster or wax. Using the model as a guide, Lipchitz would cast a larger sculpture out of bronze or carve it out of stone.

Artist Profile

René Magritte
1898-1967

René Magritte (rə nē´ mə grēt´) was born in Belgium at the end of the nineteenth century. After studying art in Brussels, he worked briefly in a wallpaper factory. The influence of his time at this factory is sometimes evident in his patterned paintings. Magritte had a mischievous attitude, and displayed an avant-garde, poetic energy. He directed this energy into numerous creations and was honored with retrospective exhibitions in both Europe and the United States.

About Art History

Surrealists valued fantastic, absurd and poetic images. They also valued the artwork of children or the untrained amateur artist because they were thought to create from pure impulse and to be free from convention. Although Magritte did not paint in a childish hand, he was a contemporary of fellow surrealist artists Joan Miró, André Breton, Jean Arp, Salvador Dalí, and Paul Eluard. In both group and solo exhibits Magritte's work was shown in galleries in Brussels, Paris, New York, and London, and is represented in many museums.

About the Artwork

The poetic nature of language interested Magritte, and he admired the way it combined with a visual image to make viewers question the context and intent of his paintings. *La Vie des Aire (The Voice of Space)* seems to ask these questions. Its floating spheres and landscape contradict reason and tell a story that cannot be easily read. Magritte didn't abandon realism in his paintings but transferred realistic objects, such as a tree, chair, or clock, into a dreamlike environment or behavior. In *The Fall* he painted men wearing overcoats and bowler hats falling from the sky onto a town below. Pattern and a muted palette make their way into a number of Magritte's works as well as some of his commissioned murals in Brussels.

About the Media

Magritte worked with oil paints on canvas.

About the Technique

Magritte employed free association in the philosophical interpretation of his paintings. He would make sketches of his subjects and then use light brushstrokes on his canvases to create a dreamlike airiness.

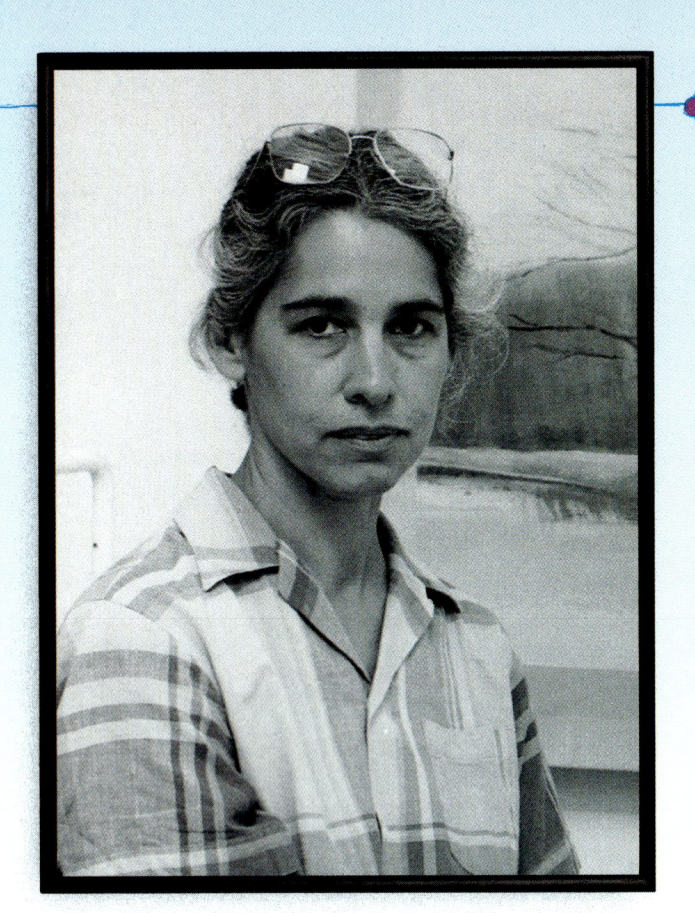

Artist Profile

Sylvia Plimack Mangold
b. 1938

Sylvia Plimack Mangold (sil´ vē ə pli´ mak man´ gōld) was born in New York City. She attended several art schools and earned a degree in fine arts from Yale University. In 1974, she had her first show, and her work has been much admired ever since. Mangold taught at the School of Visual Arts in New York City. She is married to artist Robert Mangold, and they have two sons. She lives on a 150-acre farm in Washingtonville, New York.

About Art History

Mangold's work has been called realistic. However her work does not fit easily into a specific category because her realistic paintings still have an abstract quality.

About the Artwork

Mangold's artwork reflects her surroundings. Early in her career, she painted images of floors and rooms. Later she painted scenes outside the studio window on her farm. Since 1983, Mangold has painted landscapes around her home. She has made many paintings of trees, often making a single tree the focus of a painting.

About the Media

This artist works in oils on canvas and linen and in watercolors, acrylics, pencil, ink, and pastels. She also creates prints.

About the Technique

Mangold tries to make her paintings seem three-dimensional, like sculptures. She uses rulers and masking tape while creating her paintings. She often leaves the used tape on the canvas as part of the picture. Mangold usually sketches her subjects outdoors and completes the paintings in her studio.

Artist Profile

Albert Marquet
1875–1947

Albert Marquet (äl ber´ mär kā´), the only son of a railway clerk, was born in Bordeaux, France. When he was only 16, he went to Paris to study art at the École des Beaux-Arts. Marquet experimented with new styles of painting, and during the early 1900s his works gained popularity. Marquet traveled more and more as he grew older, painting scenes from cities across Europe and northern Africa.

◀ **Charles Camoin.** (French). *Portrait of Albert Marquet.* 1904.

Oil on canvas. $36\frac{1}{4} \times 28\frac{1}{2}$ inches (92 × 72.5 cm.). Musee National d'art Moderne, Centre Georges Pompidou, Paris, France.

About Art History

Marquet first studied under Gustave Moreau at the École des Beaux-Arts. Although Moreau taught classical styles of painting, he encouraged his students to develop their own styles. Matisse also studied at the École, and he and Marquet became good friends. At that time artists such as Cézanne were moving away from the influence of impressionism and were trying to show the world as they experienced it. Marquet and Matisse became known as *fauves*—"wild beasts"—who favored self-expression and intense, bright colors, but Marquet's paintings varied greatly from those of Matisse.

About the Artwork

Marquet's painting style developed quickly and did not change much throughout his career. His greatest concern was always the relationship of the parts to the whole; details such as facial features were not his focus. Marquet created landscapes, portraits, and quick sketches of ordinary people. Even when it was not the subject, the landscape of Paris influenced his paintings.

About the Media

Marquet primarily used oil paints, pencil, and India ink. After 1925 he began to experiment with watercolors.

About the Technique

Unlike other artists of his time, Marquet always worked from nature. He did not try to reflect reality, but rather created it anew. Gradually he abandoned bright colors and began using large, free brushstrokes, using black lines to create harsh outlines.

Artist Profile

Henri Matisse
1869–1954

Henri Matisse (än´ rē ma tēs´) was the son of a middle-class couple in the north of France. He was not interested in art while he was in school. After high school his father sent him to law school in Paris. When he was 21 an appendicitis attack changed his life. Because he had to spend a long time in the hospital, his mother brought him a paint box to help him pass the time. Matisse eventually convinced his father to let him drop out of law school and study art. Matisse married and started a family soon after. His paintings were not selling, so he worked for a decorator and his wife opened a hat shop. During the last years of his life he suffered from arthritis. Unable to hold a brush in his hands, he devoted his efforts to making paper cutouts from papers painted to his specifications, and he created fantastic, brightly colored shapes. Unlike many other artists, he was internationally famous during his lifetime.

About Art History

In 1905, Matisse and his friends exhibited a painting style that showed strong emotionalism, wild colors, and distortion of shape. They were called *les fauves,* or "the wild beasts," and they experimented with intense, sometimes violent colors. Without letting their work become abstract, Matisse and other fauvist painters tested the bounds of reality.

About the Artwork

Matisse painted still lifes, room interiors, and landscapes. His paintings of dancers and human figures were generally more concerned with expressive shapes than an accurate representation of anatomy.

About the Media

Matisse painted primarily with oils, and also created many prints. Later in life he worked with cut paper.

About the Technique

Matisse worked with bold, intense colors. He simplified and distorted shapes for expressive qualities. He was most interested in the way visual elements were organized.

Artist Profile

Harrison Mc Intosh
b. 1914

Harrison Mc Intosh (ha′ rə sən mak′ ən täsh) was born in Vallejo, California, and studied ceramics at the University of Southern California and the Claremont Graduate University. His career has been predominantly based in California, where he has worked as a professional studio potter in Claremont since the mid-1950s. He also creates ceramic and glassware designs with his wife Marguerite for large factories such as the Japanese company Mikasa.

About Art History

Mc Intosh has been perfecting his talent for well over half a century, exhibiting his works in galleries and museums around the world, and his vessels and sculptures are in the permanent collections of over 40 international museums, including the Renwick Gallery of the National Museum of American Art, the Museum of Fine Arts in Boston, the Los Angeles County Museum of Art, the American Crafts Museum in New York, and many museums in Europe and Japan.

About the Artwork

As seen in *Stoneware Vase #661*, Mc Intosh often hand paints geometric designs on his vessels and uses earth tones in his palette. He creates work that reflects his interest in classic, subtle designs. He strives for simplicity in his elegant forms, and paints each ceramic piece in patterns and shapes that complement the lines of its form.

About the Media

Mc Intosh creates stoneware ceramics thrown on a wheel. These stoneware pieces are made from different types and colors of clay. They are painted with different metal oxides before their initial firing, and then they are glazed and fired again.

About the Technique

Each of Mc Intosh's creations begins as a lump of soft clay that he vigorously kneads and works to ensure that it has no air pockets before he throws it on the potter's wheel. After it is on the wheel, Mc Intosh uses the momentum of the spinning clay to slowly pull it up and out, forming a bowl, or vessel. When the vessel reaches its intended shape, it is then left to slowly dry until it is leather hard, at which time it is trimmed to refine the form. After the piece has been left to dry thoroughly, Mc Intosh paints it and then fires it in his kiln at a lower temperature than the final firing, which occurs after the piece is glazed. This final firing occurs in the kiln at very hot temperatures for long periods of time.

Artist Profile

Piet Mondrian
1872–1944

Piet Mondrian's given name was Pieter Cornelis Mondriaan, but he liked to be called Piet Mondrian (pēt môn´ drē än). He was born in the Netherlands to a Calvinist family. At a young age Mondrian could not decide between studying religion or art. He finally decided he wanted to be a painter, but his parents wanted him to be a teacher. He studied to be a teacher and later studied art at the Amsterdam Academy. Mondrian attended evening art classes and worked during the day painting portraits and copying older paintings at museums in Amsterdam. During his life, Mondrian traveled around Europe and lived in many places. He moved to New York City in 1940 to escape the war and died there in 1944.

About Art History

Mondrian carried abstraction to its furthest limits. He sought to expose the basic principles that underlie all visual images. With Theo van Doesburg he founded a magazine named *De Stijl*. In it he explained his theories of a new art form he called *neoplasticism*. He said art should express only the universal absolutes that underlie reality. Mondrian was one of the most influential twentieth-century artists. His theories altered the course of painting and had a profound influence on architecture, industrial design, and graphic arts.

About the Artwork

Mondrian painted in many different styles. As a young artist he sat on riverbanks and painted many different landscapes. After a visit to Spain his style changed. He began to order and repeat objects, and experiment with color in his paintings. He rejected all sensuous qualities of texture, surface, and color, reducing his palette to flat, primary colors. When he moved to New York City in 1940 his style became freer and more rhythmic, such as in *Broadway Boogie-Woogie*, which he painted in 1942.

About the Media

Mondrian worked in oils on canvas.

About the Technique

Mondrian wanted to create balance in his paintings. He was interested in relationships among different colors, lines, and shapes. He did not use many colors in his paintings. He generally painted with the primary colors of blue, red, and yellow and the neutral colors of black and white. He depended on his feelings to tell him when a work was complete.

UNIT 1 • Lesson 2
UNIT 3 • Lesson 2

Artist Profile

Henry Moore
1898–1986

Henry Moore (hen´ rē mor) was born in Castleford, England. When he was ten, he told his father he wanted to become a sculptor. At 18, he left home to join the army during World War I. He began studying art after the war. By age 23, he was a serious sculptor.

About Art History

In the 1930s, many sculptors were producing realistic works. However, Moore and a few of his artist friends started creating sculpture that was more abstract. Moore simplified human figures and emphasized carving forms. He used holes in his sculptures, which he associated with the mystery of caves. His early works show the influence of Mexican and African carvings. Many critics consider Moore the greatest English sculptor of the 1900s.

About the Artwork

Moore frequently combined his figures with shapes and textures from nature. He focused on making the simplest form of the subject he carved. Moore thought of his large sculptures as part of the open air with the sky as the background. Families were an important subject of his sculptures. His own family inspired his work.

About the Media

Moore carved some sculptures in wood and some in stone. Most of his large sculptures were cast in bronze.

About the Technique

Moore collected pebbles, flint rocks, shells, animal bones, and old, weathered pieces of wood for his studio. These pieces inspired him to draw. From his sketches, he made small models for his sculptures, then he made larger models. After much planning he was ready to make the actual sculptures.

● Artist Profile ●

Jesús Moroles
b. 1950

Born in Texas to Mexican immigrant parents, Jesús Moroles (hā soos´ mo rō´ lēz) creates monumental sculptures from granite, or "living stone." He has been working with granite since 1980 and now has his own successful studio headquarters—Moroles, Inc.—in Rockport, Texas. Moroles's sculptures have been exhibited all over the world, and he has had great success from the very beginning of his career. Often more than 20 feet tall, his massive creations can be found in numerous museums, as well as in outdoor environments such as the CBS Plaza in New York City, the White House sculpture gardens, the Edwin A. Ulrich Museum in Kansas, and the Albuquerque Museum in New Mexico. In 1996, Moroles opened the Cerrillos Cultural Center (C3), an exhibition, performance, and studio space in Cerrillos, New Mexico.

About Art History

After working in Italy for a year, Moroles returned to Texas in 1980 to apprentice with sculptor Luiz Jiménez. Moroles's giant granite sculptures began earning recognition right away in his early exhibitions. In 1982, Moroles received the Awards in the Visual Arts Fellowship which established his work in a two-year traveling exhibition. Word of his talent spread, and he began making large sculptures and fountains for commissions around the country. In 1985, he received a National Endowment for the Arts Matching Grant for a 45-piece installation of sculptures and fountains in the Birmingham Botanical Gardens of Alabama. He has earned national acclaim for his artwork and continues to lecture about his work and the issue of public sculpture.

About the Artwork

Moroles's granite sculptures weave together ideas of age-old history and contemporary America. In *Georgia Stele* he evokes concepts of Earth, his Mexican American heritage, and Mayan culture by using ancient granite from Georgia in a modernized form. His sculptures can be very big; *Lapstrake,* a granite work that stands 22 feet high, weighs 64 tons, and the Houston Police Officers Memorial covers 14,400 square feet.

About the Media

When he first began creating sculptures, Moroles was told to use fiberglass that looked like stone instead of actual granite. He did not take this advice, however, because he believes that a strong spiritual connection exists between an artist and stone. The granite he uses comes from varied locations, and he works on it in his Texas studio.

About the Technique

Moroles hammers five-inch steel wedges into large slabs of granite, which cause them to split. Some of his surfaces are polished, and others are left unfinished.

Artist Profile

Gabriele Münter
1877–1962

Gabriele Münter (gä brä´ lä mün´ tər) was one of the founders of modern German expressionism. She studied in Düsseldorf, Germany before traveling to the United States for two years. She resumed her studies in Munich, Germany, where she met many artists who were developing new styles of painting. She traveled throughout Europe, spending two years near Paris, France, where she learned about innovations in French art. In 1911, she joined with other radical artists in Munich to form the Blue Rider group. She painted in secret when German expressionist art was outlawed. After World War II she continued to paint and promoted the history of the Blue Rider group.

About Art History

Gabriele Münter's art emerged in the first decade of the twentieth century. It was influenced by the radical, new styles of painting practiced in two of Europe's most important art centers—Paris, France and Munich, Germany. In Paris she experimented with color and shape. When she returned to Munich, she continued to simplify her compositions, using color to express emotional and spiritual content. She and other artists of the Blue Rider group were also interested in local Bavarian folk art and crafts. Traditional German woodblock designs were another source of inspiration. Intense and expressive color contrasts, emphatic, bold designs and broad, flat areas of color define German expressionism—a style that continues to influence European and American art.

About the Artwork

Münter painted still lifes, landscapes, and portraits. In her still lifes she used objects such as chairs, tables, flowers, and plants. Her landscapes focused on simple forms of nature.

About the Media

Oil paints are made from colored pigments mixed with vegetable oils. When they dry and harden on the canvas, they produce smooth, shiny surfaces. The oils also bind the pigments to the canvas support.

About the Technique

Münter used bold, contrasting colors when creating her paintings.

Artist Profile

Joseph Norman
b. 1957

Joseph Norman (jō´ sef nôr´ mən) was born and raised in Chicago, Illinois. He received a degree in art education from the University of Arkansas and a masters degree in Art Education from the University of Illinois. His artistic studies took him to locations such as Germany, Costa Rica and Cuba. Printing, painting, and drawing since the 1980s, Norman is a poetic realist and credits his ability to understand and analyze his work to his studies in art education. He has exhibited widely throughout the country, and his work is in collections at The Museum of Modern Art, The National Gallery of Art, and the National Museum of American Art. Norman resides in Atlanta, Georgia, where he is a professor at the University of Georgia.

About Art History

Poetic realism is an expressionist method of creating art. Instead of simply illustrating a subject, Norman strives to express the subject's deeper meaning and to instill empathy in the viewer of the work. Metaphors and symbols often play important roles in poetic realism, and the artist uses these to engage people in the philosophical message of his work. Joseph Norman wrote this poem and uses it to articulate his individual artistic expression: Wherever I am / I am a Chicago artist / and in a city cactus planted in a bed of daffodils / with no illusion of ever being mistaken for a rose.

About the Artwork

Themes of race, community, nature, and humanity are commonly found in Norman's work. In *Spanish Garden #IV* he depicts his experience with the flowers he encountered in Spain. Instead of replicating actual plants, his flowers were created in his imagination. They show his mastery of the depiction of flowers and incorporate unique shapes and elements of design. Norman's inventive flowers represent the blending of different races, ethnicities, and cultures.

About the Media

Norman works with acrylic paint and charcoal.

About the Technique

Norman regards lithography, his favorite printmaking technique, as a natural transference of information from one medium to another and as a complement to his drawings. He creates lithographs without color because he wants people to bring their own memories of color to experience the work. Unlike the painstaking process of intaglio, which is another printmaking technique, lithography affords Norman an immediate result. Acrylic paints also offer a swift visual result, and Norman likes to use them because they dry fast and leave room for changes in color and texture. He chooses to draw in charcoal because of its rich quality. Sometimes he combines charcoal with acrylic, ink, or water to achieve a different effect with the medium.

Artist Profile

Georgia O'Keeffe
1887–1986

Georgia O'Keeffe (jôr´ jə ō kēf´) was born in Sun Prairie, Wisconsin. At the age of ten she began taking private art lessons, but the thing she liked most was experimenting with art at home. By 13, she had decided to become an artist. She trained under experts and won many prizes for her art. For years she challenged the art world with her unique vision. She eventually became famous for her spectacular, larger-than-life paintings of natural objects, including flowers, animal skulls, and shells. She loved nature, especially the desert of New Mexico, where she spent the last half of her life. O'Keeffe was married to the famous American photographer Alfred Stieglitz and appears in many of his photographs. In 1997, a Georgia O'Keeffe Museum opened in Santa Fe, New Mexico. It is the first museum in the United States devoted exclusively to the work of a major female artist.

About Art History

Stieglitz promoted modern artists and photographers from Europe and America through a magazine called *Camera Work* and a gallery known as "291." O'Keeffe and the circle of artists she met through Stieglitz were pioneers of modernism in the United States. She took subjects into her imagination and altered and simplified their appearances. She expressed her emotions through her vivid paintings.

About the Artwork

O'Keeffe's artwork features bold, colorful, abstract patterns and shapes. She most often painted natural forms such as flowers and bleached bones, pulling them out of their usual environments. She never painted portraits but sometimes painted landscapes.

About the Media

O'Keeffe used oils and watercolors for her paintings. She used pastels, charcoal, and pencil for her drawings.

About the Technique

O'Keeffe worked in dazzling, jewel-toned colors. She chose unusual perspectives, such as very close up or far away. She also enlarged the scale of her subjects.

• Artist Profile •

Claes Oldenburg
b. 1929

Born in Sweden, Claes Oldenburg (kläs ōl´ dən bərg) became a United States citizen in 1953. He studied writing at Yale and art at the Art Institute of Chicago. When he moved to New York City in 1956, he felt an urge to sculpt the city, so he created *The Store*. This was a painted sculpture of clothing and food displayed as if they were in a New York shop window. In 1961 Oldenburg opened a real store in New York City and stocked it with plaster food for sale. The next year he created *happenings*—mixtures of sound, movement, people, and giant cloth objects stuffed with rags or paper. This led to his first popular art form—soft sculpture. Recently Oldenburg created metal sculptures of everyday objects, greatly enlarged. Examples of his enormous sculptures include a 29-foot-long teaspoon, and a 7-foot-long typewriter eraser.

About Art History

Oldenburg was a leader of the pop art movement in the 1960s. He wanted art to celebrate life and to make people more aware of everyday objects. He wrote, "I am for an art that takes its lines from life itself, that twists and extends and accumulates and spits and drips, and is heavy and coarse and blunt and sweet and stupid as life itself." Sometimes he exaggerates the characteristics of an everyday object, changing it into an abstract form.

About the Artwork

Oldenburg is famous for giant sculptures that he creates from steel or soft materials like stuffed canvas. He sculpts ice-cream cones, electric plugs, hamburgers, lipstick tubes, and other everyday items. He built a 45-foot-tall steel clothespin in Centre Square in Philadelphia, Pennsylvania. He often makes soft, collapsing sculptures of hard items such as typewriters, toilets, and drum sets to draw attention to the form of the real items.

About the Media

Besides soft and hard sculptures, Oldenburg creates drawings, watercolors, and prints of the subjects of his sculptures.

About the Technique

Oldenburg draws his subjects before sculpting them. His soft sculptures are cut from canvas, sewn, stuffed with foam rubber, and painted. His large metal pieces are built in foundries devoted to creating sculpture from his models and whose employees work under his supervision.

Artist Profile

Pablo Picasso
1881–1973

Pablo Picasso (pä′ blō pi kä′ sō) was born in Málaga, Spain. He did poorly in school but his father, an art teacher, taught him to draw and paint. Picasso learned quickly. When he was only 14 he had a painting accepted for an exhibition. Picasso moved to Paris, France when he was 18. At the time he was very poor. Thieves stole what little he had, yet they left his now valuable drawings. In time the outgoing Picasso made many friends. Among them were the American writers Ernest Hemingway and Gertrude Stein and the Russian composer Igor Stravinsky. Picasso painted at night and slept late most mornings. He worked hard his entire life. He completed 200 paintings the year he turned 90.

About Art History

Picasso was one of the most influential artists of the 1900s. He experimented with many styles and created new ones. He invented the style known as cubism. He took 18 months to paint his first cubist picture, *Les Demoiselles d'Avignon,* which shows five women from several angles. Other artists were soon copying his style.

About the Artwork

Picasso's paintings changed as his life changed. When he was poor, he painted sad pictures in shades of blue. This style is called his *Blue Period.* When he fell in love with a neighbor, he painted happier pictures in shades of pink. This style is called his *Rose Period.* Then came his cubist period, and later he painted in a style that reminded viewers of Greek sculpture.

About the Media

Picasso created drawings, oil paintings, ceramic pieces, sculptures, prints, and engravings. He also invented collage along with the French artist Georges Braque. They combined colored papers, newspaper, old illustrations, and small objects with painting and drawing to produce collages.

About the Technique

In his cubist paintings, Picasso simplified his subjects into circles, triangles, and other basic shapes. He often outlined these shapes in black or a bright color.

Artist Profile

Maurice Prendergast
1859–1924

Born in St. John's, Newfoundland, Maurice Prendergast (mär ēs´ pren´ dər gast) was raised in Boston and began his artistic career painting naturalistic landscapes. He followed the avant-garde art movement of the Ashcan School from Philadelphia to New York, where he experimented with color theory and the depiction of the individual amidst an impersonal city. In his fifties and sixties, Prendergast wanted to create a style all his own, using a modernist freedom of color and form. This desire led him to create the large, expressive seaside paintings for which he is most famous.

▲ **Maurice Prendergast.** (Canadian/American). *Summer, New England.* 1912.

Oil on canvas. $19\frac{1}{4} \times 27\frac{1}{2}$ inches (48.9 × 69.9 cm.). Smithsonian American Art Museum, Washington, D.C.

About Art History

Impressionist painting in Paris, France, during the 1890s influenced Prendergast's early watercolors of parks and beaches. At the turn of the century he joined the Ashcan School, a group of artists who painted contemporary life in New York, and believed there should be an art movement in America separate from that in Europe. The other artists in this group, known as *The Eight,* were Arthur B. Davies, William Glackens, Ernest Lawson, George Luks, Everett Shinn, John Sloan, and founder Robert Henri. From his experience with The Eight, Prendergast developed a decorative, semi-abstract style that evolved from impressionism. In 1907, he traveled to Paris where he was inspired by the work of Paul Cézanne and Henri Matisse, and he adopted other ideas about color and abstract form. He began using these modernist ideas in his work and continued to do so for the rest of his career.

About the Artwork

After 1900, Prendergast spent more time painting the city life of New York. As his work evolved, he focused on depicting seaside parks that he felt represented an ideal world where opposites were reconciled and civilization merged with nature. These seascapes were often similar to fairy tales, with stylized, mysterious figures resting in beautiful sunlight. The figures in *Summer, New England* embody this mysterious, peaceful nature and are painted in the expressive colors of the artist's modern palette. He painted the vibrant water, trees, and figures in the same stylized manner, and this technique detaches them from reality and flattens the depth of the composition.

About the Media

Prendergast's earlier park and riverside paintings were watercolors, and his later works were done with oil paints.

About the Technique

Prendergast painted in a style called *impasto* and used the paint tube as a paintbrush and applied the paint in dots or patches directly from the tube. This gave his paintings the patchwork appearance for which his paintings are well known. His compositions were usually created in horizontal zones, full of rich color and surface texture.

UNIT 3 • Lesson 6

Artist Profile

Francesca Puruntatameri
b. 1965

Francesca Puruntatameri (fran´ ches kə poor´ oon tat ə mer ē) is from the Tiwi Islands, which are located off the northern shore of Australia. Before pursuing painting and traditional artistry, and like the majority of Tiwi artists who work in other professions prior to becoming artists, she worked in a bank, bakery, and library. The Tiwi Islands have three main art centers, and Puruntatameri works at the Munupi Arts and Crafts Association, which was formed in 1990. She uses her painting to express a cultural and social link between her heritage and her life today.

About Art History

Before European colonization in the late 1700s, Australia was inhabited by aborigines for 40,000 to 50,000 years. Creation stories are important to aboriginal culture and provide an explanation of the foundations of aboriginal social life, rules of behavior and consequences for violations against aboriginal law. Aboriginal art seeks to represent these creation stories of the "dreamtime" and to keep ancestral tales fresh in people's memories, passing them down through each generation.

About the Artwork

Traditional symbols are an integral part of contemporary aboriginal art. Ancestral designs allow an artist to continue his or her connections with their country and belief in the *Dreaming*, a series of creation stories that explain the origin of the universe. These markings often resemble designs used in body painting or tattoos and hold ceremonial significance. Bright colors and repetitive patterns, especially dots, are prevalent in aboriginal artwork, and many artists depict animals on colorful backgrounds, which help to tell ancient cultural stories. Puruntatameri's painting *Muniti Red Snapper* displays a type of fish eaten by the Tiwi people. The fish's head symbolizes the clan's hunters, and the divisions of the fish's tail represent the other members of the Aboriginal clan.

About the Media

Puruntatameri paints with gouache, a thick and opaque relative of watercolors. Gouache colors have a vibrant intensity different from luminous watercolors, but like watercolors, they perform best on thick paper and can be thinned to a fluid consistency. When wet, gouache can be scrubbed and scratched, a perfect medium for energetic paintings and sketches.

About the Technique

The straight lines and crosshatching often seen in aboriginal art are created without the aid of a straightedge or any other tool. Aboriginal artists learn their crafts at an early age and often develop their own personal symbols to display in their works.

Artist Profile

Henri Rousseau
1844–1910

Henri Rousseau (än rē´ ro͞o sō´) was born in a small town in France. When he was young he played the clarinet. He also spent some time in the French army. At the age of 25 he moved to Paris, where he spent most of his life. For a long time he worked as a customs clerk. He never went to art school. He learned to paint by practicing in gardens around the city.

◀ **Henri Rousseau.** (French). *Myself* (detail). 1890.
Oil on canvas. $57\frac{1}{2} \times 44\frac{1}{2}$ inches (146 × 113 cm.). National Gallery, Prague, Czech Republic.

About Art History

Because Rosseau had no formal art training, he is classified as a self-taught artist. The elements of fantasy and mystery in many of his paintings influenced the art movement of surrealism in the 1920s.

About the Artwork

Most of Rousseau's paintings look unlike anyone else's. In his first paintings he portrayed people and places around Paris. His most famous paintings are exotic portrayals of deserts and jungles. Many include wild animals, such as lions and monkeys. Rousseau often painted pictures of people from faraway countries. His paintings are known for their details. In some he painted every leaf on every tree and every whisker on every animal. Many of his paintings evoke the same feelings as strange dreams.

About the Media

Rousseau generally worked in oils on canvas. He mixed his colors well to make them look smooth.

About the Technique

Many people wondered where Rousseau got the ideas for his paintings. He told them that he had visited Mexico, but that was not true. He actually painted his jungle pictures by looking at the plants in the Paris botanical gardens. The animals were inspired by pictures he saw in books. He used dolls as models for people. Rousseau painted shapes very carefully to make his subjects look real.

Artist Profile

Antonio Ruíz
1897–1964

Antonio Ruíz (an tōn´ yō roo ēs´) was born in Mexico City. He grew up in an educated family that also appreciated the arts. His grandfather was a painter, his mother a concert pianist, and his father a physician. As a child, Ruíz loved to play with construction sets. After studying art in Mexico, he moved to California, where he designed movie sets. After two years he returned to Mexico to paint and to direct children's theatre. In time, he became the director of Mexico's School of Painting and Sculpture. Ruíz also taught scenery design at the University of Mexico.

About Art History
With his wit and sophistication, Ruíz helped pull Mexican art away from ancient folklore and into the modern era. He also was influential in the area of scenery design. He designed the sets for many plays and movies.

About the Artwork
Ruíz's paintings often tell a story. For example, *The Orator* shows a small man standing on a huge chair, talking to pumpkins. In *The Shop Window*, a Mexican peasant couple gaze at blonde mannequins modeling swimsuits in a store window. The contrast between the mannequins and the peasants reflects differences between the two cultures. In his later years, Ruíz painted neat, precise pictures on small canvases, which he called *postal cards*.

About the Media
This artist painted in oils.

About the Technique
Ruíz painted slowly, completing only three or four paintings in a year. His studio was on the upper level of his house, where he would shut himself off from the world for hours. He spent so much time painting that he did not like to part with a finished piece.

Artist Profile

Miriam Schapiro
b. 1923

Miriam Schapiro (mir´ ē əm shə pir´ ō) is an American artist who was born in Toronto, Canada. She grew up in the Flatbush section of Brooklyn, New York. Her parents encouraged her pursuit of a career in art and sent her to art classes at the Museum of Modern Art. She met her husband, artist Paul Brach, while attending college. They married in 1946 and have a son who is a writer. Schapiro organizes her home life so that art is woven into it. She can move from baking in the kitchen to painting in her studio and back to the kitchen without feeling interrupted. Her husband says that she has learned to live a "seamless life."

About Art History

In the beginning of Schapiro's career, her work was abstract expressionistic. Later she became an important leader in the feminist art movement of the early 1970s. She wanted art to speak as a woman speaks. In art history, women's art has been hidden. Even the materials that women have used—lace, fabric, tea towels, ribbon, sequins, buttons, rickrack, yarn, silk, cotton, and so on—have been left out of art history.

About the Artwork

In time, Schapiro's work became more geometric and structured. In the 1950s, she expressed her identity by including feminist themes in her art. In 1972, Schapiro and other female artists changed an old Hollywood mansion into a totally female environment and called it "womanhouse." Schapiro and Sherry Brody made *The Dollhouse*—a construction of bits of fabric and tiny household objects meant to reflect female life and fantasy. Schapiro also made "femmages." She invented this word to describe art made with techniques that women traditionally use, such as sewing, embroidery, piecework, and appliqué. *Femmages* are collages that reflect female emotions and creativity.

About the Media

Schapiro uses fabric scraps, sequins, buttons, threads, rickrack, spangles, yarn, silk, taffeta, cotton, burlap, wool, and other materials a person might use in daily life.

About the Technique

Schapiro uses collage, assemblage, and decoupage to join materials.

Artist Profile

Joe Seaweed
1910-1983

Joe Seaweed (jō sē´ wēd) was a Native artist of the Kwakwaka'wakw nation of the coast of southeast Alaska, British Columbia, and Washington State. Originally, *Seaweed* was spelled *Siwide* (sē´ wē dē), and meant "recipient of the paddles." The Siwides put the canoe paddles away as fishers returned with their catch. Willie Seaweed, Joe's father, was one of the most inventive Northwest coast native artists of his time. Joe Seaweed created work almost identical to his father's, and the two worked together in the village of Blunden Harbour, British Columbia. His work is part of many private collections, and is often placed alongside his father's.

About Art History

Native masks were traditionally worn in performances, ceremonies, and religious gatherings. They were also used in displays at a clan member's funeral. Each native mask carries a specific meaning depending on its image, creator, and the story it tells. Seaweed's *Mask of the Moon* was worn in a performance house and identified its wearer as the full moon. The story accompanying it narrates an argument between the crescent moon and the full moon over which moon is responsible for bringing the greater number of eulachon to the mainland rivers. *Eulachon* are small fish that are highly valued as food and a source of oil. They live in the deep waters of coastal straits, and every year they move up the mainland rivers to spawn. The fish are aided in their journey by the rising of the tides, which are at their highest when a new moon and full moon appear in the lunar cycle.

About the Artwork

Seaweed's *Mask of the Full Moon* provides a mask for the performer's face as well as a small sculpture above it that represents the moon. Smooth contours and precise grooves mark the eyes and cheekbones in the mask, and thick black bands indicate eyebrows, a beard, and a mustache. The bright red lips and nose stand out against a shining white background. The moon's symbol appears with flat, stylized markings for facial features.

About the Media

Mask of the Moon is made of red cedar, red cedar bark, mink pelts, and plywood. Red, green, white, and black paint emphasize its dynamic expression.

About the Technique

Seaweed carved his masks and creations with a variety of tools and followed his father's innovative use of a compass for circular shapes. Carving, whittling, sanding, and painting were required to create *Mask of the Full Moon*. The inside of the mask is just as smooth and precise as its outside surface. It is hollowed out in clean lines that mirror its features on the front.

Artist Profile

Gilda Snowden
b. 1954

Gilda Snowden (gil´ də snō´ dən) was born in Detroit, Michigan. She decided at a young age to become an artist and attended art school at Wayne State University in Detroit. Early in her career she made genre artwork that celebrated her life and the people around her. In 1987, both of Snowden's parents died. This tragedy changed the direction of her artwork. Her art gained depth and purpose. Snowden still lives in Detroit. She is an associate professor at the Center for Creative Studies College of Art and Design.

About Art History

Snowden uses abstract expressionistic techniques. She follows her impulses when applying color to her canvases. Instead of controlling her hands as she paints and draws she lets them move freely. This technique results in unpredictable, abstract works of art. Snowden uses this technique because she feels that the world is unpredictable. She believes she can express this unpredictability in her work.

About the Artwork

Snowden groups her artwork into three categories: *Tributes, Tornadoes,* and *Self-Portraits. Tributes* are sculptures dedicated to her family and friends. They reflect her memories of, or feelings for, these people. *Tornadoes* are paintings that radiate whirlwind energy. Her *Self-Portraits* are similar to the *Tornadoes* in style, but the forms on the canvases vaguely resemble a head and shoulders.

About the Media

Snowden creates her *Tributes* out of plywood and a variety of found objects, including photographs. To these she applies wax and paint. Her two-dimensional art is made of charcoal and pastel on paper and oil paint on canvas.

About the Technique

Snowden creates her *Tributes* by piling layer after layer of objects, wax, and paint onto a plywood base. Sometimes she includes mysterious letters and symbols. In her *Tornadoes* and *Self-Portraits,* Snowden uses sharp strokes of color moving in different directions. She likes to apply black, reds, purples, and blues to a solid background color.

Artist Profile

Frank Stella
b. 1936

Frank Stella (frangk ste´ lə) was born in Malden, Massachusetts, in 1936. He studied painting at Phillips Academy and majored in history at Princeton University. He supported himself after college by painting houses. He moved to New York City, where he had his first successful show called *Sixteen Americans*. At the age of 23, he was the youngest artist in the show. At first people were annoyed and shocked by his style. However, his talent was noticed by a few important gallery owners and critics who felt his work was exciting and new. Later in his life he became an architect.

About Art History

Stella began to paint at the end of the influential period of abstract expressionism. He is not an emotional painter like Jackson Pollock. Instead, Stella wants to paint *essential art*. This means reducing painting to strict geometric designs. He belonged to a group of artists called the "hard-edge" painters. This group used geometric shapes and little color in their works.

About the Artwork

Stella's first exhibited works were black pinstripe paintings. This style paved the way for minimalism. In the 1960s he experimented with bright colors and oddly-shaped canvases. He produced many series of paintings. One of the best known is the *protractor series,* which is made of large circles, half circles, and bright colors. In the late 1970s he combined his earlier expressionistic style with three-dimensional canvases that project nearly two feet toward the viewer's face.

About the Media

Stella uses oils, sometimes with a metallic finish. In building huge, painted canvases, he uses wood to prop up his paintings.

About the Technique

Stella's work is painted freehand. He begins by drawing guidelines on the canvas. He then fills in the space between the lines with paint. He leaves the white canvas showing between bands of paint. Sometimes he uses canvases in *U* and *L* shapes.

Artist Profile

George Sugarman
1912–1999

George Sugarman (jorj shu´ gər mən) was born in New York City in 1912, however, he did not begin to paint until 1950. The following year he went to Paris, France, on the G.I. Bill to study sculpture with the Russian-born sculptor Ossip Zadkine. He was inspired to develop his own unique style of wood sculpture. He returned to New York City and had his first exhibition in 1960. By 1969 he was one of the most celebrated sculptors in the United States. He had many one-man shows and won many awards and grants for his artwork.

About Art History

George Sugarman was one of the first sculptors to consider the negative space around his sculptures part of the sculpture itself. Because of this, he thought about gallery and museum spaces while creating his artwork. In the 1960s, critics thought this technique was experimental and daring. Today many artists, including sculptors, painters, and performance artists consider gallery spaces as they create their works.

About the Artwork

Sugarman created enormous, sprawling forms from laminated wood. His sculptures have unexpected curves and zigzags, which reach into the spaces around them. Sugarman used his sculptures to explore his ideas about space. He was interested in filling gallery and public spaces in unique ways. One technique he used was to create sequences of small forms that wandered over the length of a gallery but still seemed like one unified piece.

About the Media

Sugarman created his sculptures out of wood. Some of his artwork is covered with polychrome, a water-resistant, glossy paint.

About the Technique

Sugarman worked in an expressionistic manner when planning his sculptures. His shapes are playful, improvised, and often unexpected. Critics find some of his sculptures remarkable because they look like they do not touch the floor for support. Sugarman was a master at bending wood into the shapes he desired.

Artist Profile

Agnes Tait
1894–1981

Agnes Tait (agʹ nəs tāt) was born in New York City in 1894. She studied art there at the National Academy of Design. Until the Great Depression, Tait was able to show her work regularly. However, with a poor economy, people did not buy art. Through the Works Progress Administration (WPA), thousands of people, including artists, were given jobs, and Tait was able to continue painting. In 1943, funding by the WPA ended. Tait moved to Santa Fe, New Mexico, to live in an artists' colony. She was later recognized for her illustrations in children's books.

About Art History

The Works Progress Administration was created to put unemployed people to work. It provided jobs so that people could continue to support themselves. It employed almost nine million workers before it ended in 1943. Among its workers were painters, sculptors, and printmakers. They produced work on and inside government buildings across the United States. Nearly 10,000 paintings, sculptures, and drawings were produced through the WPA.

About the Artwork

Before the Great Depression, Tait painted still-life pictures of flowers and animals. During the Depression, her work changed to depict people and places. While supported by the WPA, she followed its guidelines to make pictures that reflected the positive aspects of American life.

About the Media

Tait often used oil on large canvases, which were usually several feet in height and width.

About the Technique

Tait's paintings express moods and emotions. To convey a cold feeling, she used hues of blue. To indicate the time of day, she adjusted the color of the sky. Her style was simple and straightforward, yet detailed.

Artist Profile

Rufino Tamayo
1899–1991

Born in Oaxaca, Mexico, in 1899, Rufino Tamayo (roō fē´ nō tə mī´ ō) was orphaned at the age of 12 and sent to live with his aunt in Mexico City. He began taking art lessons at the age of 16 and spent most of his time drawing. This caused his aunt to remove him from school and put him to work as a vendor in her fruit business. She hoped the move would encourage the young Tamayo to concentrate on other things, but he continued to draw—now using the fruit as his subject. This indomitable passion for art was evident throughout Tamayo's career, as he emphasized the universality of painting and the importance of artistic freedom.

About Art History

In 1921 at the age of 22, Tamayo was appointed head of the Department of Ethnographic Drawing at the Museo Nacional de Arqueología, Mexico City, where he was employed to draw pre-Columbian objects in the museum's collection. He had his first show in New York in 1926 and received his first of many mural commissions in 1932. His belief in the universality of painting put him in direct opposition with other well-known Mexican artists who thought painting should reflect Mexican revolutionary ideas. These muralists included Diego Rivera, Jose Orozco, and David Siqueiros. In 1936, Tamayo moved to New York City where he taught at the Dalton School in Manhattan and worked extensively on his painting and printmaking. He was eventually recognized as a master painter, even by the Mexicans who had rejected him. The Rufino Tamayo Museum of Contemporary Art was opened in Mexico City in 1981.

About the Artwork

Tamayo's early drawings of pre-Columbian art influenced the subject matter of his paintings for the rest of his career, and his style referenced that of his Mexican contemporaries and modern European painters. He also was influenced by his native land and people, and this is reflected in his intense palette of muted, earthy colors.

About the Media

Tamayo painted primarily in oils on canvas.

About the Technique

In many of his paintings Tamayo's earthy colors are textured or appear softly mottled. He achieved this appearance by using short, expressive brushstrokes.

UNIT 3 • Lesson 3

Artist Profile

Joaquin Torres-Garcia
1874–1949

Joaquin Torres-Garcia (wäh kēn´ tor´ res gär sē´ ä) was born in Uruguay. His family moved to Spain when he was 17 years old. An eager student and deep thinker, he studied many subjects, including art. As a young man, Torres-Garcia illustrated magazines, created murals, and taught art classes to support himself. In 1915 Torres-Garcia designed wooden toys with interchangeable parts to amuse his three children. He moved to New York City, where he hoped to sell the toys. However, they were difficult to manufacture. After trying to sell his toys in Italy, Torres-Garcia and his family settled in Paris. He began to use abstract primitive figures in his paintings and sold many of them. He then moved back to Uruguay and opened a successful art school. He also wrote and published articles and books, including an autobiography.

About Art History

Torres-Garcia helped found Cercle et Carre (Circle and Square), a group of artists in Paris. The group held exhibitions and published reviews of abstract art. In his own work, Torres-Garcia combined elements of the ancient pre-Columbian art of South America with elements of modern European art.

About the Artwork

Early in his career, Torres-Garcia painted realistic landscapes and murals. In time his work became more abstract and was organized by vertical and horizontal lines. Torres-Garcia filled his paintings with signs and symbols representing people, places, and ideas. He even invented his own alphabet and used it in some of his work.

About the Media

Torres-Garcia worked in oils, watercolors, and ink. He also created murals, wooden sculptural pieces, and toys.

About the Technique

Torres-Garcia was fascinated with structure. He used lines and color to organize his paintings. Sometimes he drew grids over his paintings to divide them into sections.

Artist Profile

Patricia Walker
b. 1949

Patricia Walker (pə tri´ shə wô´ kər) was born in Natrona Heights, Pennsylvania, which is located near the Allegheny River. She received her degree in painting from the Rhode Island School of Design in 1985. In 1987, she completed her master of fine arts degree in painting at Cornell University. Since the fall of 1987, she has enjoyed teaching fine arts at Georgia Southern University.

About Art History
Walker has been influenced by many artists including Henri Matisse and Willem de Kooning. What intrigues her about these artists is the way they broke down flat spaces with abstracted backgrounds, figures, and objects.

About the Artwork
Walker paints many still lifes with objects and parts of figures in abstracted spaces. The use of abstraction in her work reflects an emotional and psychological place that is enhanced further by her choice of colors. Many of her paintings show fragmented images of body parts. Much of her new work deals with the entire human figure.

About the Media
Walker works in pastels, charcoal, or gouache. She frequently makes pencil drawings that are as large as five feet by four feet. She paints with oils on canvas or on rag paper.

About the Technique
Walker often starts her work with an image in mind, usually an abstract composition. She slowly develops elements of shapes and patterns into images. She views painting like assembling a jigsaw puzzle with many shapes that must be manipulated until they all fit together.

Artist Profile

Arapaho Man's Shirt

An unidentified Arapaho Indian artist made this shirt around 1890. The women of Native American Plains tribes usually made clothing for members of their families. Their designs were mostly abstract and geometric, and the patterns in these designs were often balanced.

◀ **Artist unknown.** (United States). *Arapaho Man's Shirt.* c. 1890.
Buckskin and feathers. 37 inches (93.68 cm.) long.
Buffalo Bill Historical Center, Cody, Wyoming.

About the Artwork

This Arapaho shirt was worn during a ritual performance called the *ghost dance*. The ghost dance became a part of Arapaho culture around 1888, when many Arapaho people were forced from their homes and relocated to reservations. The ghost dance was performed during ceremonial prayer sessions, where the Arapaho asked for blessings and for the ability to return to their tribal way of life—free of interference from other cultures.

About the Media

This shirt is made of buckskin, paint, and bird feathers.

About the Technique

The crow design painted on this shirt symbolizes the traditional Arapaho belief in the crow as a messenger from the spirit world. The stars also represent the spirit world. The shirt's formal balance is evident in the way the symbols are arranged symmetrically.

Artist Profile

Bridal Bed Cover

This bridal bed cover was made during the nineteenth century by an unknown Japanese artist. It was designed and crafted as a wedding gift to a young Japanese couple. The expensive materials used to create these bedcovers, as well as their beauty and grandeur, made them symbols of the wealth and social status of the bride's family. Because these bedcovers were so delicate and valuable, they were carefully stored or displayed as wall hangings, not used as everyday household items. Thanks to this gentle treatment and protection from bright light, these textiles have retained their original colors for hundreds of years.

◀ **Artist unknown.** (Western Japan). *Bridal Bed Cover.* Nineteenth century.

Rice paste resist, painted pigments, plain weave cotton. 76 × 61¾ inches (193.04 × 156.85 cm.). Museum of International Folk Art, Santa Fe, New Mexico.

About Art History

Largely due to pressure from the Western world, Japan ended its policy of national seclusion in 1853. This allowed a flood of social, cultural, and artistic influences from around the world to enter the country, resulting in many changes to the artwork of Japan.

About the Artwork

Every image and symbol on the cover had significance to the bride and groom, conveying their families' wishes for their happiness in marriage and a long life together. The family crest of the bride, within the white circle near the top of the cover, is symbolic of her family's wishes for protection for the couple. The long tasseled rope is a depiction of an ancient Shinto sacred rope, the *shimenawa,* which is used to ward off evil and to indicate a sacred area of the gods within a worship hall or shrine. Evenly spaced along the rope are pairs of white fern fronds, symbols of purity and the happiness of marriage. The six lobsters that appear are traditional Japanese symbols of happiness and longevity.

About the Media

Woven cotton, indigo and other fabric dyes, and rice paste were used to create this cover.

About the Technique

The resist technique used to create the images on *Bridal Bed Cover* is called *tsutsugaki.* A paste made of rice flour and water is applied to dry fabric using a cone-shaped applicator tube. The outlines of a design are created with the rice paste, and dyes are used to color inner portions of the design. More paste is applied over parts of these colored portions, and then the entire cloth is dipped in liquid indigo dye. Once the fabric has dried, the hardened rice paste is scraped off, revealing a colorful design outlined in white.

UNIT 1 • Lesson 4

Artist Profile

Chinese Children's Slippers

These slippers were created by an elderly grandmother who sold them on a tiny side street in Shanghai, China. Embroidered clothes made for little boys are said to play a role in protecting them from evil spirits. When a child is one month old his or her mother or grandmother may make a tiger hat, tiger pillow, tiger collar, and tiger shoes, which are viewed as both shields and decorations.

▲ **Artist unknown.** (China).
Chinese Children's Slippers. 1991.

Cotton appliquéd with silk. $4 \times 2 \times 1\frac{1}{2}$ inches (10.16 × 5.08 × 3.81 cm.). Hudak Private Collection.

About Art History

Some of the most delightful pieces of Chinese folk art are textiles, and include cotton and silk embroidery. *Embroidery,* the stitched decoration on clothing and other textiles, has traditionally been one of the few ways a peasant woman could display her artistic skills.

In China, sons may represent the future of a family. They are given the responsibility for their elders and ancestral spirits. A woman may say that her son is her greatest treasure, giving birth to sons is a status symbol. As a result the textiles created especially for her sons receive a woman's deepest attention. Women from traditional China were valued not for their beauty, but for their embroidery skills. Embroidery is one of the oldest forms of artistic and decorative expression in China.

About the Artwork

These enchanting slippers were made to keep children from tripping as they first learned to walk. The little tiger faces seen on the front of these shoes were made to help scare away bad spirits and to watch over a child. Tigers are the chosen motif because they are believed to not bother human beings, but are ferocious enough to frighten away bad spirits. Traditionally, a child wears tiger clothing and sleeps on a tiger pillow on birthdays and during other festivities, such as New Year's.

About the Technique

A tiger's face is first sketched onto the slippers. Then a woman stitches the pattern into the cotton with silk thread.

Artist Profile

Corn Palace

A variety of architects, contractors, and artists have worked on the Corn Palace in South Dakota. The current building was designed by architects Rapp and Rapp of Chicago. This architectural firm also designed Radio City Music Hall in New York City and many other famous theatrical buildings in the United States. The exterior designs, changed every year, are created by different people. Five of the interior panels were designed by artist Oscar Howe.

▲ **Artist unknown.** (United States).
Corn Palace. c. 1892.
Mitchell, South Dakota.

About Art History

The first Corn Palace was built in 1892 to celebrate the fertile farmland in Mitchell, South Dakota, and to promote settlement of the area. The Corn Belt Expositions held inside the Palace were extremely successful. This success prompted larger structures to be built in 1905, 1921, and 1937. In 1937, the Byzantine-inspired minarets, turrets, and kiosks were added. During the winter months from 1919 to 1920, the dirt floor was flooded and the Corn Palace served as South Dakota's first indoor skating rink. In 1979, the Palace caught fire, but was saved by local firefighters. In 1987, the building underwent renovations costing $650,000.

About the Artwork

The Corn Palace is covered from top to bottom with native grasses, grains, and a variety of colored corn. These are arranged in attractive designs. Because of the effects of weather and hungry birds, the exterior must be changed every year. One of the permanent interior panels shows pheasant hunting, a popular pastime in the area.

About the Media

The Corn Palace is covered with thousands of bushels of dock, wild oats, brome grass, bluegrass, rye straw, and wheat, as well as other grains and corn.

About the Technique

By September of every year, the decorations are removed and a new decor is applied. Workers stand on tubular steel scaffolding and use air nailers and staplers to put up the grains, corn, and grasses. Wheat and straw are first tied in bunches. Corn is cut to the required lengths with a specially designed table saw. The total annual cost of decorating can vary from $25,000 to $60,000, depending on the amount of surface to be worked.

Artist Profile

Four Patch in Triangles Quilt

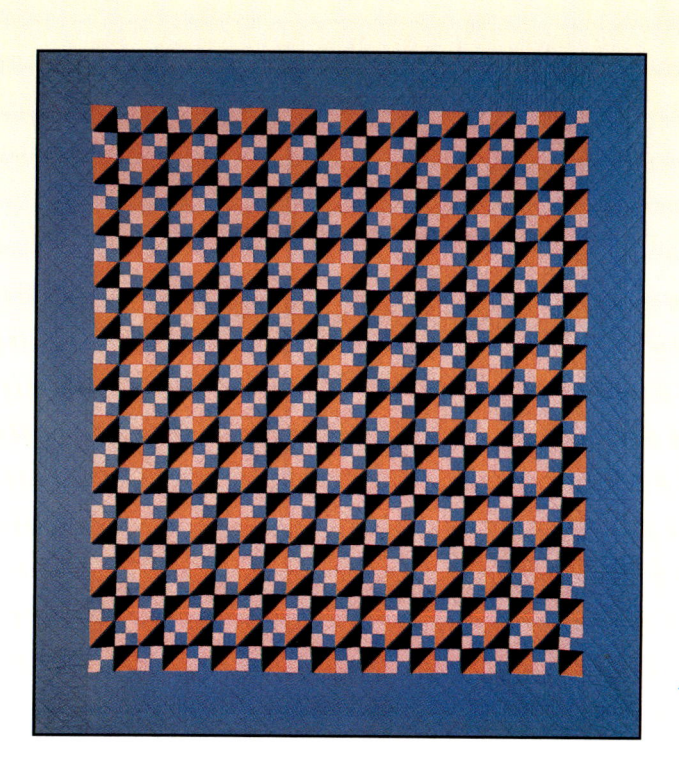

Barbara Zook Peachey belonged to a community of people who practiced the conservative Christian Amish religion and way of life. The Amish emigrated from Europe to North America during the eighteenth century and settled mainly in the Great Lakes states. The Amish believe in a simple life of devotion to God, separate from and as unaffected as possible by the modern world around them. The Amish are known for their strong work ethic and the excellent quality of the goods they produce.

◀ **Barbara Zook Peachey.** (American.) *Four Patch in Triangles Quilt.* 1910–1920.

Cotton. $85\frac{1}{2} \times 78\frac{3}{4}$ inches (217.17 × 200 cm.).
Museum of International Folk Art, New York, New York.

About Art History

Amish women are world renowned for the unique, beautiful quilts they design and sew by hand. These quilts are so well made that if they are gently used and cared for they can be passed down through many generations as family heirlooms. In Amish communities, quilts are made and given as gifts for special occasions such as weddings and the birth of children. The Amish did not bring the tradition of quilting with them from Europe but learned the craft from their neighbors after settling in North America. Amish quiltmakers have developed their own methods, styles, and patterns, which have been passed down to younger generations within their communities.

About the Artwork

This quilt is a classic example of a traditional Amish geometric-patterned quilt. This quilt's maker, Barbara Zook Peachey, was a member of the Yellow-Topper Amish, also known as the Byler Group, which used colored fabrics for quiltmaking. Mrs. Peachey was able to include colors in her quilt that may not have been permitted by the laws of more conservative Amish groups.

About the Media

This quilt is made of cotton cloth.

About the Technique

The construction of a quilt begins with the collection of many small scraps and cuttings of fabric that the women save when making clothing. When the quilt design and pattern have been determined, the scraps are cut into the desired shapes and then stitched together for what will become the quilt's top layer. When the top layer stitching is complete, a bottom layer is sewn to the top, with batting, fiber filling, or feathers sewn into the middle layers. Finish stitching is sometimes done from the outside as a way to keep the stuffing or layers of material from shifting within the finished quilt.

UNIT 5 • Lesson 4

Artist Profile

Hmong Story Cloth

This story cloth was made by an unknown artist of the Hmong people of eastern Asia. Ancestors of the Hmong lived along the banks of the Yellow River in China more than 4,000 years ago. Since that time the Hmong have had a difficult history of persecution, forced relocation, and migration into and out of refugee camps. The Hmong people spent many years working to establish themselves in Laos, Thailand, Vietnam, and Cambodia. Always a minority group wherever they went, they farmed the land and served in the armies of their host countries. In 1976, Hmong families began moving to the United States in search of safe places to live and work.

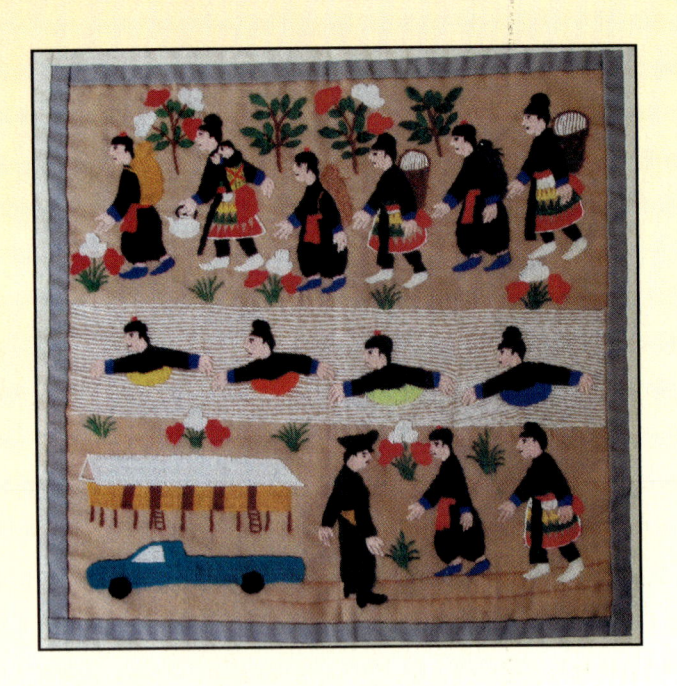

▲ **Artist unknown.** (Hmong Peoples, Asia). *Hmong Story Cloth.*

Cotton. 18 × 18 inches (45.72 × 45.72 cm.).
Private collection.

About Art History

Hmong artwork is often an interpretation of the events happening in the lives and histories of the artists' families. A traditional Hmong art form is the story cloth, sometimes called a flower cloth. These textiles are silent storytellers, often serving as the only record of a journey, battle, or other event experienced by a family or an entire village. The story cloth is an important part of Hmong culture because until the late 1950s, the Hmong language had no written form. When families or other groups were forcibly separated and dispersed, they had no way to communicate across geographic distances or to tell their stories to younger generations. The story cloth was a way for the Hmong to record and preserve their history and cultural identity.

About the Artwork

This story cloth shows a scene embroidered in colorful thread on a rose background. A narrow blue border surrounds a white outer border. All of the human figures are wearing black except for a soldier at the bottom of the scene who appears to be wearing a dark green uniform. This story cloth tells three parts of one story. Near the bottom of the cloth, two men appear to be communicating with a soldier. In the middle section, four men are swimming, and at the top, a group of six men are walking through a garden or forest carrying children and packs of supplies strapped to their backs. The specific events that inspired the creation of this scene are unknown.

About the Media

This cloth was made using three or four layers of fabric. The embroidery was done with cotton thread. The appliqué work on this cloth was completed using fabric.

About the Technique

Traditionally, men have designed the images depicted on Hmong story cloths. Men sketched designs onto the cloth, then women embroidered the detailed figures, colors, and patterns.

UNIT 5 • Wrap Up

Artist Profile

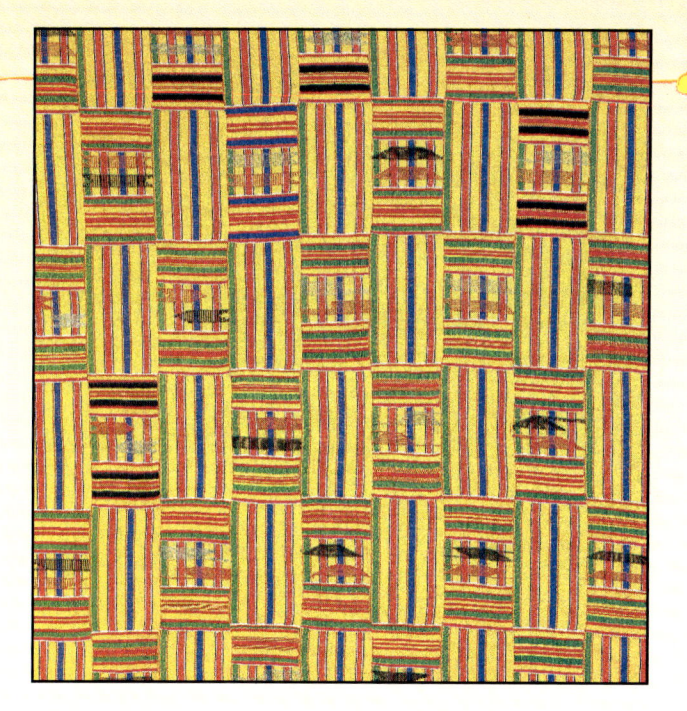

Kente Cloth

Kente cloths are made by the western African Ashanti people of Ghana and the Ewe peoples of Ghana and Togo. The weavers who make kente cloth are traditionally male. The art of weaving kente is passed down from generation to generation.

▲ **Artist unknown.** (Ashanti Peoples, Ghana). *Kente Cloth.*

Museum of International Folk Art, Santa Fe, New Mexico.

About Art History

Kente cloth has been worn by African royalty for hundreds of years to show power and prestige. The word *kente* means "that which will not tear away under any condition." Traditional kente cloth is the national costume for the people of Ghana. It is worn for ceremonial occasions, such as festivals, weddings, and births.

In traditional African societies, every piece of art must have a purpose and fulfill a need. Baskets, ceramic storage containers, musical instruments, utensils, furniture, religious icons, buildings, and articles of clothing are all enhanced by African artists.

About the Artwork

Kente cloth is dazzling and colorful. Colors such as red, yellow, and green are woven together into a pattern of lines. Each patchwork pattern is produced by the placement of colors, and each color combination has a different meaning. Red and yellow suggest life and its power over sickness; green and white, a bountiful harvest; and blue, love and the rule of the queen. Men in Ghana drape kente cloth over themselves, and women wear kente as skirts.

About the Media

Kente cloth is made of silk or cotton fiber.

About the Technique

Kente cloth is woven on narrow looms with floor pedals. The strips are cut into pieces and sewn together side by side.

Artist Profile

Letter Holder or Book Cover

This letter holder or book cover was made by an artist of the Mi'kmaq people, a Native American group located in the far northeastern coastal areas of North America. The unidentified Mi'kmaq artist who made this piece lived on the peninsula that is now called Nova Scotia. The Mi'kmaq were hunters and fishers, usually living in areas where fish were most plentiful. They were resourceful people, finding uses for every part of the animals they killed.

◀ **Artist unknown (Micmac).** (Mi'kmaq People, Nova Scotia, Canada). *Letter Holder or Book Cover.*

Birch bark decorated with porcupine quills, glass beads, and silk. $14\frac{1}{2} \times 10\frac{1}{4}$ inches (36.83 × 26.04 cm.). International Folk Art Museum, Santa Fe, New Mexico.

About Art History

Mi'kmaq artisans are probably best known for the creative use of tree bark and porcupine quills in their unique works of art. This letter holder or book cover is an example of the type of object that was painstakingly decorated with porcupine quills. The Mi'kmaq made delicate boxes, jewelry, headbands, chair backs, and fans using bark and quill weavings. Their geometric, floral, and lace-like designs are so detailed and precise that they give the visual effect of fine embroidery, similar to that done by Europeans.

About the Artwork

This beautiful, original work of Mi'kmaq art is believed to be either a covering for a book or a protective folder for storing letters. Dyed porcupine quills in white, blue, red, black, and beige have been woven through the birch bark backing in a complex, geometric pattern. Components of this pattern include triangles, squares, rectangles, and half circles. In several areas, an overlapping cross-hatching design has been used. Geometric shapes and patterns were popular with Mi'kmaq artists at the time this piece was made.

About the Media

This letter holder or book cover was made from birch bark decorated with porcupine quills, which were dyed in traditional colors.

About the Technique

A traditional Mi'kmaq technique was used to decorate this letter holder or book cover. Porcupine quills were soaked in water until they became soft and flexible. Perforations were made in the birch bark using an awl or other sharp instrument. Both ends of the softened quill were threaded down through the perforation and then bent together on the underside of the bark. The holes through which the quills were threaded were small enough to firmly anchor the quills in place.

UNIT 5 • Lesson 1

Artist Profile

Man's Headband of Toucan Feathers

This headband was made by unidentified Shuar people from Ecuador. Ecuador is part of the Amazon basin. The Amazon covers an area of about six million square miles and extends into nine countries—Peru, Brazil, Ecuador, Colombia, Bolivia, Venezuela, French Guyana, Guyana, and Surinam. Five hundred different tribes live in the Amazon. Each tribe has its own language, beliefs, and customs. Today Amazonian tribes continue to work to preserve their cultures.

◀ **Artist unknown.** (Ecuador).
Man's Headband of Toucan Feathers.

Cotton, feathers, human hair, and thread. Courtesy of the Smithsonian National Museum of the American Indian, New York, New York. Photo by David Heald.

About Art History

The Shuar live in the eastern lowlands of Ecuador. They created an organization known as the *Federacion Interprovincial de centro Shuar-Achuar.* Part of the group's mission is to be sure that museum collections represent these tribes as a living, vital culture in the Amazon region. Because both tribes still exist, they do not want museums representing them as if they are no longer viable.

About the Artwork

Feathered headbands are worn as symbols of bravery and authority by older men and political leaders in the Shuar tribe. Usually headbands are worn only during celebrations and other special occasions. This headband is a woven cotton band decorated with red and yellow toucan feathers and black feathers from a bird called *awacha*. The headband has danglers that look like earrings. These are made from toucan feathers and human hair.

About the Media

This headband is made of cotton, feathers, human hair, and thread. Tools needed to create a headband include a loom and a needle.

About the Technique

To create a headband such as this one, the cotton band is woven on a loom. Then feathers and human hair are sewn on for decoration. Hair is taken only from living people who volunteer to cut their hair as a contribution to the headband.

Artist Profile

Mola

The Kuna live on the islands of the San Blas Archipelago off the eastern coast of Panama. In the sixteenth century, they were an important culture and lived in central Panama. Now the fewer than 40,000 remaining Kuna live in small villages. Most families earn a living by farming or fishing, but some people commute to Panama City to make money.

▲ **Artist unknown (Kuna).** (Panama). *Mola.*
Layered and cut fabric with stitchery. Private collection.

About Art History

Molas are only one form of Kuna art. Recently drawing has become an important part of Kuna history and life. Although the Kuna like their lifestyles and are trying to resist change, the Kuna culture is quickly becoming more modernized. They want to preserve their past, but they have no written language except for sacred hieroglyphs, so they are capturing their culture by making picture stories. These pictures are being collected in archives so future generations will know how the Kuna lived in the past.

About the Artwork

Mola is the Kuna word for cloth. Molas are decorated with decorative panels on the front and the back. The complex, bright designs reflect Kuna beliefs, daily activities, and the environment around them. They show plants, birds, animals, and themes from Kuna mythology or the Bible. The patterns are abstract and based on the general shapes that Kuna find in the coral in the ocean around them.

About the Media

The Kuna make their molas from cloth bought in Panama City or island shops. They also use needles, thread, and scissors.

About the Technique

Mola appliqué requires a cloth base and a covering layer of a contrasting color. The top layer is partially cut away to reveal shapes and color underneath. Additional layers of cloth may be inserted beneath the top layer, and small patches of cloth sewn on the top layer. Sewing is done by hand and machine. Lines of chain stitching—a type of embroidery—are used to decorate uncut areas of cloth.

Artist Profile

Ngady Amwaash (Mweel) Mask

This mask was made by an unidentified artist of the Kuba peoples of the Democratic Republic of the Congo, formerly known as Zaire, located in central Africa. The Kuba is a large confederation of approximately nineteen different ethnic groups living in central Africa. The ancient Kuba kingdoms were wealthy and rich in cultural traditions, myths, and legends. The Kuba people are known for their skills in metalwork, woodcarving, and sculpture. Traditionally, men and women in Kuba culture practice different art forms.

◀ **Artist Unknown (Kuba).** (Democratic Republic of the Congo). *Ngady Amwaash (Mweel) Mask.* Date unknown.

Wood, paint, glass beads, cowrie shells, string, raffia, cloth. $12\frac{1}{2}$ inches (31.75 cm.) high. Virginia Museum of Fine Arts, Richmond, Virginia.

About Art History

During the late nineteenth and early twentieth centuries, Europeans became increasingly fascinated by African artwork. Many Europeans brought works of African art home, and there were eventually large public and private collections throughout Europe. Unfortunately some of the art history of the Kuba was lost due to turbulent years of Portuguese and Belgian control.

About the Artwork

This mask is one of the ten types of Kuba masks that have been identified by art historians and anthropologists. It is believed that this type of mask, also called *Mweel,* was introduced by Queen Ngokady of the first Kuba dynasty in celebration of the role of women in Kuba culture. It is possible that the face on the mask represents an important female ancestor of the Bushoong Kuba dynasty of the seventeenth century, perhaps Queen Ngokady herself. This mask was worn by male dancers during ritual dances that reenacted parts of Kuba history and mythology.

About the Media

This mask is made of wood, cloth, raffia palm fiber, shells, and glass beads. The white cowrie shells adorning the mask have special significance because the color white is symbolic of death and mourning in Kuba culture.

About the Technique

This mask was hand carved from hardwood. The cloth portions were woven, and shells, beads, and raffia fibers were stitched onto the cloth.

Artist Profile

Plaque

This plaque was made of hammered gold and was found in a burial site near the skull of an important local chief. The plaque was made in Cocle, a province of central Panama on that nation's southern coast, sometime between 700 and 1100 A.D. The individual artist is unknown, but this plaque is typical of Cocle work during this period.

▲ **Artist unknown.** (Panama). *Plaque.* 700-1100 A.D.

Gold. $8\frac{2}{3} \times 8\frac{1}{2}$ inches (22 × 21.6 cm.).
The Brooklyn Museum, New York, New York.
Peabody Museum Expedition to Cocle Province, Panama.

About Art History

Art objects created by the indigenous people of Cocle were discovered on and off from about 1850. In 1915, archaeologists figured out that one local culture had created the art. Formal excavations began in 1925. From 1930 to 1933, extensive work was done in Cocle. Archaeologists found artifacts made of gold, copper, and other metals. Some items were carved out of bone or ivory. They also found textiles and pottery. All of the artifacts were found at burial sites. The plaque shown here was found during a 1931 archaeological dig conducted by Harvard University. The excavation was funded by the Brooklyn Museum.

About the Artwork

This plaque shows an image of a creature that seems half human and half reptile. It has big eyes, sharp teeth, and claws on its hands and feet. Crests shoot out of its head. Images commonly found in Cocle artifacts resemble fish, frogs, birds, monkeys, and human heads and bodies. Some images are completely abstract.

About the Media

The artist used gold to make this plaque.

About the Technique

The goldsmith hammered the metal to a thin sheet, then embossed designs on it with a hammering tool. The artist must have worked over a soft surface, such as leather or sand, to make the image rise above the surface of the metal.

Artist Profile

Potawatomi Turban

The Potawatomi people were farmers, fishers, hunters, and trappers. They traveled by horse and navigated the rivers in birch bark canoes. Originally from the Great Lakes area, the Potawatomi had a tribal alliance with the Ojibwe and Ottawa peoples known as the Council of Three Fires. During the Indian Removal Act of the 1830s, American troops forced the relocation of the Three Fires peoples to territories in the central plains states. Some Potawatomi fled to Canada to escape the removal. Populations of Ojibwe, Ottawa, and Potawatomi still live in Kansas, Oklahoma, and the Great Lakes regions of the United States and Canada.

◀ **Artist unknown.** (United States). *Potawatomi Turban.* c. 1880.

Otter pelt, silk ribbon, glass beads. $6\frac{1}{4}$ inches (15.88 cm.). Chandler-Pohrt Collection, Detroit Institute of the Arts, Detroit, Michigan.

About Art History

The Potawatomi carved enormous canoes from tree trunks, made dome-shaped homes and woven baskets from the bark of birch trees, fashioned cooking utensils from mussel shells, made bear-claw necklaces, and created various musical instruments using the skin, bones, and hooves of the animals they killed for food. They sewed beadwork designs onto the leather of their moccasins, and adorned women's skirts and shawls with colorful ribbons and silver brooches. Dyed porcupine quills and glass beads were used to decorate deerskin clothing. Instead of wearing feather headdresses as the men of other tribes did, Potawatomi men wrapped their heads in turbans made of fur.

About the Artwork

This turban is crafted from otter skin and beadwork. Made to fit close to the wearer's head, the turban measures about seven inches in height. The hand-beaded symbols adorning the turban were outlined in white and filled in with blue, green, yellow, red, and pink.

About the Media

The Potawatomi used animal hides to make clothing. Deerskin was used to make moccasins, shirts, dresses, and leggings. Buffalo hides were used for heavy cloaks and winter outer garments. This turban is made from the fur and skin of an otter. The turban is decorated with glass beads and silk ribbon, materials obtained by trading with other tribes or neighbors of European origin.

About the Technique

Animal hides were scraped clean of flesh and then stretched and tanned to preserve the leather. Tanning also kept the hide soft and supple, making it a good material to use for clothing. The beadwork was stitched onto the otter fur after the tanning process was complete.

Artist Profile

Ritual Figure

This figure was created during the twelfth dynasty of the Middle Kingdom of ancient Egyptian history. The statue might have been carved by one artist and then painted by another, or it might have been designed and constructed by a larger group of artisans. Little is known about the individuals and groups who created portrait sculptures such as this one, but it is presumed that they enjoyed some degree of recognition as respected members of their communities.

◀ **Artist unknown.** (Egypt). *Ritual Figure.*
c. 1962–1928 B.C.

Gessoed and painted wood. Height $22\frac{7}{8}$ inches (58.10 cm.). The Metropolitan Museum of Art, New York, New York.

About Art History

Sculptors of the Middle Kingdom began to assert a bit more creativity of style and form than their predecessors. Especially in the creation of portrait statues, the Middle Kingdom sculptors added a depth of emotion, personality, and expression to portraits that was not seen in earlier works. Though they were carved from wood and stone, fine details were added so that the eyes and faces of these statues seem to reveal the thoughts and innermost feelings of the persons they represent.

About the Artwork

This figure was a portrait of a member of an Egyptian royal family living during Dynasty 12 of the Middle Kingdom. Portrait carving was a common way of honoring royalty in ancient Egyptian culture, and many of these portrait statues have been found inside the tombs of the nobles. The name of this particular nobleman is not known, but his royal status is evident by the presence of the staff, headdress, and jewelry.

About the Media

Sculptures from the Middle Kingdom period were often carved from stone, such as black granite, but some were made of a dense hardwood. This figure was carved from hardwood and then coated with a gesso preparation.

About the Technique

Evidence shows that ancient Egyptian sculptors worked in teams when creating large works such as the relief sculptures found on the walls of tombs. This figure is much smaller; it was carved and painted by an individual or a smaller group of artists. Because Egyptian craftsmen were influenced by established artistic traditions, this statue was created through a set process and style that changed little over thousands of years.

UNIT 4 • Lesson 4

Artist Profile

Seated Arhat

This statue was made by an unknown Chinese artist during the late Yuan dynasty or early Ming dynasty. Portraits of arhats were a popular art form during these time periods. Because many sculptors engaged in the creation of these graceful statues, it has proven difficult for art historians to identify the specific artist who created this piece. Inscribed on the back of this statue are the names of the donors who commissioned the work, as well as the name of the temple that was to receive it as a gift.

◀ **Artist unknown.** (China). *Seated Arhat.* c. 1300–1450.

Cast iron, traces of pigment. Height $30\frac{11}{16}$ inches (77.95 cm.). Kimbell Museum of Art, Fort Worth, Texas.

About Art History

Small statues of arhats were prevalent in the art of India, Tibet, and China during the fourteenth and fifteenth centuries. The statues often portray groups of four, 16, or 18 arhats together. The Ming dynasty is most famous for its elegantly beautiful porcelain ceramics, but artists of this period also produced wonderful paintings, textiles, architecture, furniture, jewelry, and sculpture.

About the Artwork

This statue was created in China during the late Yuan or early Ming dynasty. This work is a portrait of a religious figure known as an arhat, or *lohan,* a member of a group of highly respected monks who were disciples of Shakyamuni Buddha. Arhats were believed to possess superhuman powers attained by reaching the highest levels of Buddhist spirituality.

About the Media

This statue is made of cast iron. Originally the statue may have been painted, because traces of pigment remain on its surface.

Artist Profile

Sioux Moccasins

These moccasins were made around the turn of the twentieth century by an artist who belonged to the Sioux tribe. The part of North America that is today the states of Minnesota, North Dakota, South Dakota, and Nebraska was once the land of Plains Indians tribes, such as the Sioux, Absarokee, Kickapoo, Sauk, Fox, Hidatsa, and many others. The Plains peoples hunted buffalo and other animals, often following migrating herds over long distances. In the mid-nineteenth century, the Sioux way of life was threatened, and the people were in danger of starvation as settlers and those heading west for the California Gold Rush killed off most of the buffalo on Sioux lands.

▲ **Artist unknown.** (United States). *Sioux Moccasins.* c. 1900.

Cowhide, rawhide, porcupine quills, glass beads, metallic beads, cotton fabric, tin cones, and dyed horsehair. $10\frac{3}{4}$ inches (27.3 cm.). Detroit Institute of Arts, Detroit, Michigan.

About Art History

Artwork has always been an important part of the Sioux culture. In addition to beautiful beadwork Sioux artists have developed unique styles for making elaborately patterned quilts and clothing. They decorated their buffalo hide teepees with images and symbols, and some of them told stories about the history of the tribe.

About the Artwork

Moccasins are soft leather shoes that traditionally have been worn by many different Native American peoples. They vary greatly in appearance—from simple, plain, slipper-style shoes to extremely ornate and heavily beaded shoes that were worn for special occasions. These beautifully adorned and fringed moccasins were probably worn during ceremonial dances.

About the Media

These moccasins are made of leather, rawhide, cotton cloth, porcupine quills, glass and metal beads, tin, and horsehair.

About the Technique

Long ago Sioux women began making beads by cutting dyed porcupine quills. Later some women began to trade with Europeans for glass beads. They sewed beads to their saddlebags, clothing, and moccasins in short rows, producing geometric designs. The symbolic meanings of these designs varied.

UNIT 6 • Lesson 4

Artist Profile

Standing Youth

This statue was created in China during the Eastern Zhou dynasty. This time period, spanning the late fifth to the early fourth centuries B.C., is known today as the *Warring States* period. No information as to the identity of the artist has been found.

◀ **Artist unknown.** (China). *Standing Youth.* Late fifth–early fourth century B.C.

Cast bronze with applied jade. Height 11¾ inches (29.85 cm.). Boston Museum of Fine Arts, Boston, Massachusetts.

About Art History

During the Eastern Zhou period, artists began to display an interest in creating more finely detailed and lifelike sculptures and statues of the human figure, especially in the portrayal of facial expressions, clothing, hair, and ornamentation. This *Standing Youth* is a good example of the type of statues produced by the artists of this period. The care with which his clothing, boots, and braided hair were sculpted, as well as his intent gaze and expression of fixed concentration, demonstrate the artist's eye for realistic detail.

About the Artwork

This sculpture is larger than many other bronze sculptures from this time period, location, and culture. The statue represents a young man, possibly a performer or an animal trainer, looking at one of two birds sitting on top of the large rods, or sticks, he has grasped in his hands. The style of hair and clothing on the figure has led some historians to believe that this youth may have been a member of the Xiongnu minority group, or even a nomad from the northern regions of China. This sculpture is part of a collection of small statues found in an ancient Chinese tomb.

About the Media

This sculpture is made of bronze, a copper-based metal alloy, and jade, a green gemstone.

About the Technique

The figure of the youth and the two large sticks were cast in bronze. The two birds perched on top of the sticks were carved from small pieces of jade.

Artist Profile

The Dwell House

The Dwell House model was designed by a California design group called the Central Office of Architecture. The COA began in 1987 as the dream of three architects: Ron Golan, Eric A. Kahn, and Russell N. Thomsen. These three men wanted to start an architectural firm that was dedicated to creative, quality design work. The COA has prided itself in its ability to find practical, innovative solutions to problems that arise when planning or building a new structure. The San Francisco Museum of Modern Art is home to a permanent exhibit of some of the COA's unique works.

▲ **Central Office of Architecture.** (Los Angeles, California). *The Dwell House.* 2003.

Dwell. July/Aug. 2003 page 80.

About Art History

A prefabricated house, often referred to as a *modular*, is a structure that is constructed by assembling large, previously built sections on location. Because a prefabricated house is partially completed at the time on-site building begins, it requires far less time, fewer workers, and fewer materials than building a traditional house. Prefabricated houses became popular in the United States after the end of World War II, when men and women returning from overseas created a huge demand for affordable, single-family homes.

About the Artwork

The Dwell house was the Central Office of Architecture's design submission to a competition called "The Dwell Home Design Invitational," sponsored by *Dwell* magazine. The competition challenged architects and designers to submit detailed plans for an original, modern, affordable, environmentally friendly prefabricated house with a construction budget of $175,000. When designing the house, the COA architects used elements of many different types of structures as inspiration. For example, the sloping steel roof was inspired by the metal canopies used at covered gas stations. The house design features prefabricated cabinets, wall panels, and roof canopy.

About the Media

The Dwell house's main components are steel, concrete, and glass.

About the Technique

The Dwell House is still a model for prefabricated houses. If the structure were built, it would begin with the digging and laying of a post-tension concrete slab for a foundation. The steel and concrete skeleton of the house would be built over the foundation, then the prefabricated components including the walls, cabinets, and roof canopy added.

Artist Profile

The Thinker

Created by an unknown artist over six thousand years ago, *The Thinker* was found in an excavated gravesite of the Neolithic Hamangia peoples of Cernavoda, located in what is today the nation of Romania.

◀ **Artist unknown.** (Hamangia Culture, Romania). *The Thinker.* 5500–4700 B.C.

Clay. Height $4\frac{1}{2}$ inches (11.43 cm.). Natural History Museum, Bucharest, Romania.

About Art History

The culture of the Hamangia people is categorized by historians as a Middle Neolithic culture. This means that the Hamangia was a society of the Stone Age, having developed during the second half of the sixth millennium B.C., and continuing for a thousand years. Peoples of the Stone Age used stone tools for many purposes. It is assumed that clay statues and sculptures such as *The Thinker* were formed with the aid of sharpened, stone hand tools.

About the Artwork

The Thinker is made of clay, although art historians have commented that the piece has the look of very ancient wood. The male figure of the thinker appears to be seated upon a low, four-legged stool. His arms, bent at the elbows, rest on his knees, and his hands cradle his face. This pose, along with the somewhat serious expression on his face, gives him the look of a man deep in contemplation. A small statue of a kneeling female form was found near *The Thinker*. This female figure, created with identical materials and in the same style as *The Thinker* statue, may have been a representation of the thinker's wife.

About the Media

The Thinker was made using *loam,* or clay, found in the area where the piece was made.

About the Technique

The exact method used to create *The Thinker* is not known. It is assumed that the statue was formed by hand and then detailed using a small hand tool. Because the piece is in excellent condition thousands of years after it was made, it is thought that this figure was fired or baked to set the clay.

Artist Profile

Tortilla Molds

These tortilla molds were made by an unknown artist from Vizarrón, a town in the central Mexican state of Querétaro. Although the identity of the particular artist who carved the three molds shown here is not known, the location of their origin narrows the list of possible artists to those living within Vizarrón during the 1930s.

◀ **Artist unknown.** (Mexico). *Tortilla Molds.* c. 1930.

Carved wood. Approx. 10 × 2 inches (25.4 × 5.08 cm.). San Antonio Museum of Art, San Antonio, Texas.

About Art History

Tortilla molds are often made exclusively in Vizarrón, Querétaro. Tortilla molds are used to decorate the hand-made tortillas served with meals at special events, such as family reunions and religious celebrations.

About the Artwork

Tortilla molds are carved with patterns, designs, and images that have patriotic and religious meaning to the people of Vizarrón, Querétaro. Because corn flour tortillas are a staple of the Mexican diet, they are included in most meals, from humble family breakfasts to festival banquets. As cooks and families prepare for a special occasion, such as a religious celebration or family party, decorative patterns and images are pressed into the otherwise plain tortillas to give them a festive appearance. This makes eating the tortillas seem more special, and their beautiful patterns and designs add to the décor of the celebration.

About the Media

These tortilla molds were carved from the wood of the mesquite tree, which is native to Mexico.

About the Technique

Tortilla molds such as the three shown here are hand carved from a hard wood, usually mesquite.